MW01489857

Marrying the Right One

Marrying the Right One
By
Dr. Don Woodard

Light Keeper Publications
PO BOX 490
TROUTVILLE, VA 24175
Liferelationships.net

Copyright 2024
Donald Noel Woodard Sr.

All Scripture Quotations from the
King James Bible

Word Definitions from the Websters 1828
Dictionary of the English Language
Noah Webster
Unless otherwise noted

Contents

Introduction..7

Finding Whom Your Soul Loves......................9

The Purpose of Marriage.........................19

Is It Too Late for You?.........................27

Create Your Own World.............................29

Expectations Part One (For Men)..................39

Expectations Part Two (For Ladies)..............51

In-Laws and Out-Laws............................59

Thoughts on The Song of Solomon................69
 (By: Bill and Roberta Taylor)

Thirty Pieces of Silver..........................73

Important Questions to Ask Yourself............79

Holy and Beautiful.............................133

Toy or Treasure................................137

Wedding Vows...................................149

Prayers, Dreams and Time (A Poem).............151

The Best Relationship..........................153

Special Thanks to Bill and Roberta Taylor for their input and assistance with this project.

https://successful-marriage.blogspot.com

And to Mrs. Wendyjo Householder
Hope4TheHurting.org

Introduction

"Marrying the Right One" is a revision and I believe an improvement of a book by the same title I wrote in 2010.

In 2016 I attended a conference, while there I heard one of the speakers make a comment about relationships, the comment sparked in me a passion to study relationships in the Sacred Scriptures. I've learned that "Life is About Relationships," your most important relationship in life is your relationship with God through His only begotten Son, Jesus Christ. Your second most important relationship is your relationship with yourself and if you're married your third most important relationship is with your spouse. Whom you marry is the second most crucial decision you will ever make in life.

I'm still learning, my desire is to be a disciple, a learner of truths and principles that I can share with others to help them improve their lives.

The purpose of this essay is to help people prepare themselves for the second most crucial decision in their life, to make sure they know about the most crucial decision in their life and improve their relationship with themselves.

Living in HIS grace,

Don Woodard

Finding Whom Your Soul Loves

The watchman that go about the city found me: to whom I said, Saw ye him whom my soul loveth? 4) It was but a little that I passed from them, but I found him whom my soul loveth: I held him, and would not let him go... Song of Solomon 3:3-4

Whom you marry is the second most important decision you will make in life, second to believing on Jesus Christ as your Saviour. Marriage is the third most important relationship you will have in life. Your most important relationship being your relationship with God through His only begotten Son Jesus Christ and the second being your relationship with yourself.

The purpose of this book is to help you take a careful look at choosing a spouse and making the second most important decision in life in an informed manner.

The following are some things I've learned and some observations that I pray you will find helpful toward finding whom your soul loves.

Some things I've Learned

I am old enough to have watched people grow up. I watched my own generation come of age, and

I've seen the fruits of those who sowed their wild oats and watched as they grieved over their harvest.

I have seen young people, even those who had godly parents and a concerned pastor, walk away from everything they knew to be right, only to regret later the life of becoming a prodigal. I have also seen people experience disaster in life's second most important decision—choosing whom they would marry. My desire in writing this book is to keep people from experiencing heartache in choosing a spouse.

When it comes to ministering to teenagers and young adults, I think we become so focused on helping them deal with the immediate present that we do not always help them prepare for their future. However, if they are focused on living correctly in the present, their future will take care of itself.

The following are some facts about life that I trust will be helpful to you.

Life is the sum total of all the decisions we make.

At the time of this writing, I'm sixty-four years old. A large part of everything I am, the situation in which I live and the condition of my life at this present moment are the results of decisions I have made up to this point. Yes, God blessed me with parents, good friends, concerned pastors along the way, and other positive influences; but I made the decisions on what I did with all of those blessings. So, my life is now the sum total of the decisions I have made, just as your life will be when you are approaching thirty, forty, fifty and sixty years of age.

Victory or defeat in life has more to do with how we respond to our circumstances than with the circumstances themselves.

Life holds for us both good and bad circumstances. It will not be the circumstances that alter how things turn out for us as much as it will be what we determine to do with those circumstances.

"Show me your friends, and I will show you your future."

This is a favorite quote of my friend and former youth director, Rich Lemon, who is now in Heaven. It is also a very true and powerful statement. My friend Charlie "Tremendous" Jones often says, "You are the same today as you'll be in five years except for two things: the people you meet and the books you read."

Friendship is one of the most powerful influences you will ever have in your life, so choose your friends wisely. They will definitely be a factor in arriving at your "sum total."

**Keeping life's priorities right
will help determine how things turn out.**

We cannot let circumstances and influences determine how things are going to be done. All decisions in life must be based on principles. Principles are the priorities. Keeping God's will first in our lives is both a priority and a principle by which we should live.

**God's perfect will for
my life is that I obey Him today.**

People, especially young people, often ask me, "How do I know God's will for my life?" Or a young teenager might ask, "How do I know whom I am going to marry when I am older?" The best way to know God's will for our future is to obey God's will today, to do what we know we are supposed to be doing right now, to be obedient to the Word of God and the spiritual leadership God has placed in our lives, and to follow the Lord's leading in every way. If we focus on being obedient today, then five years, ten years, fifteen years or more down the road will take care of itself.

It is better to do things right the first time.

I have heard people say, "I'm going to try it this way, and if that doesn't work I'll just try something else." In essence, they are not searching for the very best way, that is, the right way, the first time. Then there are those who choose to do things their own way instead of God's way. They usually try to justify this in their own minds by convincing themselves that they know what they are doing by making statements like, "It's my life! I will live it my way!" The truth is, it is not your life, and you do not know what you are doing, so it is best to listen to godly counsel, seek the will of God and do things right the first time.

Six observations from sixty-four years of living.

Never give your heart too soon!

It is not wise to get emotionally involved with someone before you have had an opportunity to get to know him or her and develop a friendship. Your heart in the wrong hands can be easily crushed. Be careful whose hands you put your heart in.

Never give your heart when you are too young.

I feel this is an important observation to make for my younger teenage readers. I have had fourteen-year-old girls come to me crying and asking, "Brother Don, I'm fourteen, and I do not have a boyfriend. What am I going to do?" My gracious answer to that question is always the same: "You don't need a boyfriend at the age of fourteen!"

I fear that many parents and others who influence young people have put undue pressure on teenagers today to go "steady," or to have a boyfriend/girlfriend relationship too young. We should return to the practice of courtship beginning at the appropriate age.

So, my dear young teenage friend, I encourage you to wait for the right time. Do not give your heart when you are too young! Don't get emotionally involved with someone of the opposite sex until you are old enough to support him or her, at least!

Every emotional relationship has a positive or negative effect, or both.

In every emotional relationship, we pick up things that we might refer to as baggage. Some are positive, and some are negative. In these emotional relationships, we invest a piece of our hearts, and we create a memory. It is very important that we choose carefully the people with whom we develop close emotional relationships. This practice will prepare us for choosing the right spouse. We must guard our emotions and not entrust our hearts to people who could have a negative influence on us.

Do not seek a relationship for the sake of a relationship.

As I mentioned earlier, some parents and others in leadership positions in the lives of young people push the idea of teenagers having a boyfriend or girlfriend.

Therefore, some young people get involved in an emotional relationship with someone of the opposite sex just so they can say they are in a relationship. Then there are those who get into their twenties who feel that because of their age they should be in a relationship. These are wrong reasons to have a relationship.

Do not commit to a relationship for the sake of having a relationship. Begin a relationship because God has led you to someone and only when all the other circumstances are right in your life for you to develop that relationship.

A right relationship is about giving.

In the Garden of Eden, God gave Adam and Eve everything they needed. He gave Eve to Adam as a help meet. He gave them everything they needed to eat, and of all that God created He said, *"Behold, it was very good"* (Gen. 1:31). All that God has ever given to man has been very good.

The point is that giving is an important principle in having the right relationship with anyone. God has always sought to give to man. In seeking a relationship with anyone, our desire should be what we can give to the relationship, not what we can take.

Since I am a male, I pick on the young men. Most young men approach a relationship with a young lady with the thought of what they can get out of the relationship. This of course is natural, but it is not spiritual. The way to grow into a relationship of any kind is to ask ourselves, "What can I give this relationship?" This is what we should ask. ourselves in our friendships and in our relationships with our parents, our grandparents, our children and whom we choose to marry. Love always gives; lust always takes!

**"Don't sacrifice the permanent
on the altar of the immediate."**

This was one of Dr. Bob Jones Sr.'s often repeated. quotes. In other words, don't get yourself into a relationship now that you might regret for the rest of your life. Getting involved physically before marriage is not only a sin, but it is also sacrificing the permanent on the altar of the immediate. Having your heart broken because you got too involved emotionally with someone who was not right for you or when the timing was not right, or when the situation was not right would be sacrificing the permanent on the altar of the immediate.

You have your whole life ahead of you. God has someone very special for you, someone with whom you will develop a long, loving and permanent relationship.

Don't sacrifice all of that on the altar of the immediate!

The Purpose of Marriage

I asked a couple of friends: What is the Purpose of Marriage? Here are a few of the responses I received.

The first is from a widow lady who has a ministry to women. "Marriage brings honor to God and shows others to Christ by mirroring His love for us. Marriage gives us companionship and fulfillment. Through marriage, we replenish the earth. I spend time reminding ladies that God is a jealous God, and He wants their attention on Him first. If hubby is a companion you can trust and he fulfills you, that is "icing on the cake." But she should find her needs met through our heavenly Father first. When a woman feels she cannot trust her husband (I mean that broadly-romantically, financially, emotionally, in concerns of privacy...), it is devastating. It is devastating if she is left unfulfilled or feels she leaves him unfulfilled. She finds peace if she can wrap her head around God first."
Wendyjo Householder, Hope4TheHurting.org

The next quote is from a pastor who has been married thirty-five years, "I believe two things. One, marriage is to cure loneliness and two, for a woman to help the man. There are some things a man is not wired to do and there's things a woman is not wired to do. Put them together and they get the job done." Pastor Matt Swiatkowski

This quote is from a friend who has been married over forty years, "To determine the purpose of marriage one should begin with defining the purpose of life." Jeff Blakeman, Pastor Emeritus Bible Baptist Church Chillicothe, Ohio.

This quote is from a dear friend who is in his fifties. Sadly, his wife passed on Mother's Day in 2023. His perspective on the purpose of marriage is powerful. "I believe marriage does many things in the life of a man. Marriage teaches us to love but it also teaches us about other things that come along with that, it teaches us about lust, anger, bitterness, hurt, patience, and forgiveness. It teaches us about honesty, loyalty and that life doesn't always give us what we want. It teaches us pleasure and it teaches us about death. We all experience all the above at various times throughout our marriages. All of these, plus so many others set the stages for what I believe is one of the purposes of marriage, to make me the man that God designed me to be and to cause me to continually have to work to improve that man. To be that man that God designed for that woman. She will be working through these same things and together if we do it correctly, we as a couple will bring glory to God." Eugene Mills, Director of Sunset Ministries, Salem, Virginia

The word "Purpose" means "That which a person sets before himself as an object to be reached or accomplished; the end or aim to which the view is directed in any plan..."

What is the purpose of Marriage? What was God's purpose for men and women coming together in the marriage relationship? Let us begin by addressing the question: What is your purpose for being alive? Why did God create you? Genesis 1:26-28 says, *And God said, Let us make man in our image, after our likeness: and let them have dominion over the fish of the sea, and over the fowl of the air, and over the cattle, and over all the earth, and over every creeping thing that creepeth upon the earth. 27) So God created man in his own image, in the image of God created he him; male and female created he them. 28) And God blessed them, and God said unto them, Be fruitful, and multiply, and replenish the earth, and subdue it: and have dominion over the fish of the sea, and over the fowl of the air, and over every living thing that moveth upon the earth.* From this passage, we understand that God created man for the purpose of a relationship with Him, so that He could love man and communicate and commune with Him. Your purpose is to be one with God, to return His love, to worship Him, to glorify Him, and to introduce others to Him.

We read in Genesis 2:18-20, *And the LORD God said, It is not good that the man should be alone; I will make him an help meet for him. 19) And out of the ground the LORD God formed every beast of the field, and every fowl of the air; and brought them unto Adam to see what he would call them: and whatsoever Adam called every living creature, that was the name thereof. 20) And Adam gave names to all cattle, and to the fowl of the air, and to every beast of the field; but for Adam there was not found an help meet for him.*

Some overlook a vital statement in this passage; notice these words in verse twenty, *...but for Adam there was not found an help meet for him.* Simply stated, none of the animals God had created could fulfill Adams need for companionship or for a helpmeet. In Genesis 1:21 we see that God took a rib from Adam and created the woman. *21) And the Lord God caused a deep sleep to fall upon Adam, and he slept: and he took one of his ribs, and closed up the flesh instead thereof; 22) And the rib, which the Lord God had taken from man, made he a woman, and brought her unto the man. 23) And Adam said, This is now bone of my bones, and flesh of my flesh: she shall be called Woman, because she was taken out of Man. 24) Therefore shall a man leave his father and his mother, and shall cleave* *unto his wife: and they shall be one flesh. 25) And they were both naked, the man and his wife, and were not ashamed.* (Genesis 1:21-25)

 What is the purpose for the creation of the woman and for marriage? God gives us an essential part of the answer in Genesis 1:18, *"It is not good that the man should be alone; I will make him an help meet for him."* The first purpose of Marriage is for spiritual, emotional, and physical companionship. The second purpose is to replenish the earth with more people so that they can have a relationship with God and each other, especially the one special person that completes them in marriage.

They Shall be One Flesh

 Most young men read the words, *"...they shall be one flesh."* And think only of the physical intimacy in marriage. However, the principle of *"One Flesh"* has a much deeper and emotional and spiritual meaning. A man and woman becoming one flesh in marriage is them becoming one person in soul and body. By soul, I speak of the emotional connection and oneness they should have as their relationship becomes more romantic, even before marriage. As well as the spiritual oneness they should have through their mutual faith and relationship in Jesus Christ. The oneness of two people in love with each other brought together by God should continue throughout their married life.

How do Two People Become One?

The Apostle Paul prayed for the church at Colossi that *"...their hearts might be comforted, being knit together in love..."* (Colossians 2:2). If it's important to God that His people in the New Testament Church have their hearts be comforted and knit together in love, I suggest that it is equally if not more important for a couple becoming married, being married and remaining married have their hearts knit together in love also. How do we accomplish this in a way that a couple's hearts continue to knit together?

A man and woman must approach the marriage altar with one perfect heart to start their lives together. This begins with making the decision to love your spouse. Love is a decision! To love your spouse is a daily, purposeful commitment to a sacrificial action. The love for your spouse will flow from your love relationship with Jesus Christ.

A couple begins to be one and continues to be one by deciding daily to love, serve, have conversations, listen to, encourage, open their hearts to one another, give themselves to one another, and love and serve God together. All of this is part of the purpose of companionship in marriage.

Be Fruitful and Multiply

As discussed earlier, we find another purpose for marriage in Genesis 1:28 *"...God said unto them, Be fruitful, multiply, and replenish the earth..."* Of course, we understand this means married people should bring children into their marriage by birth or adoption.

In a Christian marriage, it is much more than bringing children into the family! It is deciding before marriage that when the children come, you will, *"...bring them up in the nurture and admonition of the Lord."* (Ephesians 6:4) and that you will, *"...love the Lord thy God with all thine heart, and with all thy soul, and with all thy might. 6) And these words, which I command thee this day, shall be in thine heart: 7) And thou shalt teach them diligently unto thy children, and shalt talk of them when thou sittest in thine house, and when thou walkest by the way, and when thou liest down, and when thou risest up. 8) And thou shalt bind them for a sign upon thine hand, and they shall be as frontlets between thine eyes. 9) And thou shalt write them upon the posts of thy house, and on thy gates."* (Deuteronomy 6:5-9)

Bringing children up to know God, to have a personal relationship with Him through Jesus Christ is a purpose of marriage, and it is the primary biblical purpose of parents.

This may seem like a lot to consider when marrying the right one, but I remind you that who you choose to marry is the second most crucial decision you will make in life, and the marriage relationship is the third most important relationship you will ever have. For these reasons, it is extremely important that you pray about whom you marry, and in praying, consider God's purpose for your life as you seek His will in marrying the right one!

Is it too Late for You?

"Therefore if any man be in Christ, he is a new creature: old things are passed away; behold, all things are become new." 2nd Corinthians 5:17

Before we continue, I want to pause and address something very important. Not everyone is brought up in a Christian home; not everyone starts out right, and not everyone has the opportunities that some of us have. Some of us have had moral failures and have had the wrong kind of relationship. Some of us have had relationships that were not biblical, and some of us have regrets.

We would agree that the biblical way is the best way. Unfortunately, that is not the way all of us take. Referring to his personal regrets and past sins, the apostle Paul wrote, *"...I obtained mercy, because I did it ignorantly in unbelief."* (1st Timothy 1:13)

Some of us have what I refer to as "relationship regrets." Things we would do differently if we could do over. There might be people we would not have a relationship with if we had it to do over again. As the apostle Paul said, we did things *"...ignorantly in unbelief."*

27

Paul also said he *"...obtained mercy."* It wasn't too late for Paul to have a productive life and it's not too late for you to enjoy your life. We have a merciful God, and Jesus is an *"...all things are become new"* Redeemer. (2nd Corinthians 5:17) He is the restoring God and the God of another chance. If you are a person with a "relationship regret", may I encourage you from the authority of Scripture? You may have had a rough start, but you can finish right!

You may have had a "relationship regret", and maybe more than one, that does not disqualify you from finding the person you want to spend the rest of your life with.

Your "relationship regret" did not rob you of the joy or the freedom to love and be loved by someone. You are not disqualified from loving and having a happy Christian marriage.

Regrets are regrets; we cannot change them, but we can learn from them, we can improve ourselves, help others learn, and move on and do better. Don't let your past regrets rob you of the life you can live now in Jesus Christ, including having a meaningful, loving relationship.

Keep the faith and finish right!

Create Your Own World

(Adapted from the author's book,
Life's About Relationships)

The Genesis account of creation begins, *"In the beginning God created the heaven and the earth."* (Genesis 1:1) The chapter continues with God creating the sun, moon, stars, the firmament, land, grass, trees, vegetation, all animal life and finally human life. This is not a detailed description of what Genesis 1:1–25 tells us, but the truth for us to focus on is that before God created man, He created a secure, fruitful world with everything that would be needed for a lasting and meaningful relationship.

God's purpose in creating man was for a relationship, Ephesians 2:10 says, *"For we are his workmanship, created in Christ Jesus unto good works, which God hath before ordained that we should walk in them."* God's purpose in creating the world was for the man to have a place to develop that relationship. Consider the wisdom in this, God did not create man then try to create a world for the man to live in. He created the world first. Here is the principle of this relationship lesson: create your world first then seek to build a life relationship. By world I'm referring to your personal life, your existence, your personality, your character and attributes. You might ask, but I have been married a while or I've been in a relationship for a while so what am I to do? My answer to that is simple: create a better world. No matter where we are in our relationships, we can always improve ourselves and we can always improve the world we are creating. D. L. Moody is credited with saying, "The biggest room in the world is the room for improvement."

The following are principles for creating your world or improving your world.

Have a Close Relationship with God

Our relationship with God is the foundation on which we build all other relationships in life. As we commented earlier, God created us for the purpose of a relationship, and He has already initiated a relationship with us by creating a world for us and giving His only begotten Son, Jesus Christ to be our redeemer. The way we complete the relationship is by humbling ourselves enough to realize that we need God and by believing on Jesus Christ as our Saviour. John 1:12 says, *"But as many as received him, to them gave he power to become the sons of God, even to them that believe on his name:"* It is turning to Jesus Christ in faith the brings us into a relationship with God, once you have that relationship   continually build and strengthen

30

your relationship with God and all other relationships in your life will begin to improve.

Know Who You Are and
Know What You Can Offer

Most of us seek what we can get out of a relationship instead of what we can give to a relationship. God offers a lot to us. God knows who He is, and He knows what He is able to offer us, in His relationship to us He offers unconditional love, communication, forgiveness, abundant life, stability, and much more that we can humanly comprehend. In return, He expects that our hearts will be perfect toward Him as David's heart was perfect toward God.

Looking at our own relationships, we must know our strengths and our weaknesses to know what we can offer in a relationship and what we must guard against distracting our relationships. The other important aspect of knowing who you are and what you can offer is that you can use this knowledge to grow and make a sincere effort to improve yourself. By doing so, your relationship's will improve.

Have a Firm Set of
Principles to Follow

When you select your life principles, consider how those principles will affect others in your life. Will your life principles enhance your relationships? Some people are deceived into thinking that something is wrong with everyone else because no one can seem to get along with them, when in fact the problem is not everyone else, the problem is them! The reason for this is they do not have a firm set of life principles to live by. If your life is not guided by firm principles, your lack of principles will manifest in your closest relationships. Seek the Bible for the best source of life principles to follow, and those principles will enhance your relationships.

Have a Clear Vision of the Kind of World You Want to Build

On October 1, 1971, five years after Walt Disney passed away, Disney World had its grand opening. During the dedication ceremony, someone turned to Mrs. Walt Disney and said, "Isn't it a shame that Walt didn't live to see this?" Mrs. Disney replied, "He did see it, that's why it's here." (Mike Vance, Creative Director at Disney) This story contains a great truth about having a vision for our lives. I certainly don't pretend that I know the mind of God, but I'm confident that God envisioned the kind of world He wanted to create for the first man before He ever created the heaven and the earth.

We must envision the kind of world we want to create for our relationships. The young adult who is searching for his or her life mate should envision the type of world they want to create for that person. Although Mr. Disney created a fairytale kind of world, the principle holds true: we should have a clear vision and a desire to create a world that will make our relationships all that they can be. What vision do you have for your closet relationships?

Create a Secure You

Most of us desire leaders that are stable and secure in who they are and where they are going. A stable person will create a stable world, and an unstable person will create an unstable world. All of us need secure, stable relationships, and if we ourselves are secure, we can help create better relationships.

Be secure in who you are emotionally by strengthening yourself spiritually. Anger, jealousy, bitterness, strife, and similar emotions will cause unstableness and will affect our relationships. If you are struggling in a close relationship, ask yourself: Am I or the other person dealing with any unstable emotional issues? If you suspect there are issues, address them.

The World God Created Has Seasons

One of the blessings of the world God created for us is the four seasons. Each new season brings change, and each season has its own beauty. My personal favorite season is spring. I love the newness of life, the grass beginning to green, the trees coming to life with leaves, the flowers blossoming, and the warming weather. As God's creation has seasons so will the world we create for our relationships.

We notice this most in our marriage relationship and in our relationship with children. My wife Debbie and I have gone through the season of our youth, we have gone through the season of rearing our children, and now we are in the season of enjoying grandchildren. In the coming years, we will enter the season of old age. Sometimes we are faced with difficult seasons. When the difficulties come, just be patient, remain focused on the person you love and weather the season you are in.

Perhaps one of the most difficult seasons our family has weathered together was the death of our grandson Caleb who died in the womb just weeks before his due date. Our family focused on my daughter and her husband with prayer, love and affirmations of God's peace and comfort. It was a difficult season for all of us but especially for our daughter. God was gracious to us and carried us through. The spring season came, and our daughter gave birth to a beautiful little girl about a year and a half later. Spring is coming!

Take Dominion of Your World

When God created man and put him in the world He had created for him, He instructed the man to *"Be fruitful, and multiply, and replenish the earth, and subdue it: and have dominion..."* (Genesis 1:28)

There are two important words here, the first is *"subdue"*, which means to conquer, and the second word is *"dominion"*, which means to control. These are some of the first instructions God gave to man, and these instructions contain some very important truths about life and about relationships.

In order for us to conquer the world we are creating; we must first conquer ourselves. And in order for us to have dominion over the world we are creating, we must have control over ourselves. A lack of control over oneself is a sure way to cause relationship challenges. When we don't have control over our personal emotions, behavior, temperament, actions and reactions then our world will be out of control and issues will develop in our relationships. The best example of this is that when the woman lost control of herself and ate of the forbidden tree. Genesis 3:6 states *"And when the woman saw that the tree was good for food, and that it was pleasant to the eyes, and a tree to be desired to make one wise, she took of the fruit thereof, and did eat, and gave also unto her husband with her; and he did eat."* We see here that woman ate the forbidden fruit because it was pleasant to the eyes and was a tree to be desired. She rejected what God had told Adam concerning not eating the forbidden fruit, she released dominion of herself and her world to the serpent that had intruded into her world. Causing she and Adam to lose control of their world and it affected their relationship with God. The consequences of this were severe, In Genesis 3:16 God told the woman, *"I will greatly multiply thy sorrow and thy conception; in sorrow thou shalt bring forth children; and thy desire shall be to thy husband, and he shall rule over thee."* Genesis 3:23 says, *"Therefore the Lord God sent him forth from the garden of Eden, to till the ground from whence he was taken."* Adam and Woman lost control over the world they had in the Garden of Eden because the lost control of themselves. Dominion of your world begins with dominion over yourself.

Maintain the World You Create

When God placed man in the Garden of Eden, He told Adam to *"Dress it and to keep it."* (Genesis 2:15) The word "dress" has the idea of work or till the ground, to serve. To maintain good relationships in our world, we must serve those we love, and we must continually cultivate our own lives spiritually. The word *"keep"* means "to hedge, guard, or protect". This is very important; we must protect the world we create. In the Garden of Eden, God had created a perfect place for man, then gave them dominion and freewill to make choices. They chose to allow the Serpent to enter into a conversation with them. Through deceit and persuasion, he was able to cause havoc and division in the relationships between Eve, Adam and God. This was Adams failure as the husband. Always protect the world you are creating, always protect your marriage and family from the enemy and his world.

Create a World That Will Replenish Itself

God said, *"Let the earth bring forth grass, the herb yielding seed, and the fruit tree yielding fruit <u>after his kind</u>, whose seed is in itself, upon the earth: and it was so. And the earth brought forth grass, and herb yielding seed <u>after his kind</u>, and the tree yielding fruit, whose seed was in itself, <u>after his kind:</u> and God saw that it was good."*
(Genesis 1:11–12)

Notice the underlined words. Every living thing that grows from the earth has some kind of seed or spore whereby it reproduces itself, after its kind.

God created the world to replenish itself after its kind. The world we create should be one that replenishes itself with love, grace, mercy, understanding, justice, hope, service, humility, patience, truth and life. For a world to reproduce these attributes, these attributes must be sown into the world created. We must develop these attributes by our own behaviors, by the way we treat those closest to us and by those we invite into our world and share our world with. In order to sow them into the lives of others, you must first have them in your own life.

What Are the Characteristics of
the World That You Are Creating?

If we realize that the world we have created is not the best it can be, we can make improvements, beginning with our own attitudes and behaviors. If you are not content with the life you are living, or the world you are creating it's not too late to make changes or improvements. Begin with improving yourself, work on your relationship with God and with yourself, you will find that your other relationships will follow, and you will also find that your world will improve.

Expectations
Part One

Marriage is a lifetime commitment between a man and a woman that have chosen to love and cherish each other for life. God expects them to work together to create a safe environment where they can nurture and admonish their children and bring them up to serve Him. Entering into marriage both parties have expectations as to what marriage will be like, as well as expectations of the other person.

Unfulfilled expectations produce disappointments and discouragement. Therefore, it's important to understand that you are going to marry a flawed human being and the person they marry is also a flawed human being. Don't enter in into marriage with the idea of your spouse making you happy but rather enter marriage with the goal of making your spouse happy by meeting their biblical expectations.

It's important that both the groom to be and the bride to be understand that God loves both of you and that God has a plan for marriage, a plan that works. God made women to be His good and perfect gifts to their husbands. Whenever a man's wife frustrates him, he must assume that these characteristics are of God to bless him. Pray for wisdom and understanding of meeting one another's expectations in marriage.

A careful reading of Ephesians 5:1-17 will help us understand that the ability for a man and woman to meet one another's expectations in marriage will flow from their individual relationship with the Lord Jesus Christ. Walking in the love of Christ will help us walk in love in the marriage relationship. I encourage you to take a few minutes and read Paul's words in Ephesians chapter five carefully before reading this section of the book.

What do we mean by "Expectations!"? More importantly, what are the expectations of marriage? Mr. Webster helps us with this definition, "A state or qualities in a person which excite expectations in others of some future excellence." Thankfully God has given us the best marriage and relationship book to learn from. In the sacred scriptures we find what a woman should expect from her husband and what a man should expect from his wife in the marriage relationship.

Since God determined the man to be the spiritual leader in the home let's begin with him.

FOR MEN

<u>Biblical Expectations of the Husband in Marriage</u>

Gentlemen, as you read through this list keep in mind each item is a biblical expectation a wife has of her husband.

1) A woman has a biblical expectation to be loved by her husband.
   Husbands, love your wives, even as Christ also loved the church, and gave himself for it; (Ephesians 5:25)

   <u>"Husbands love your wives..."</u>
   In his commentary on the book of Ephesians Albert Barnes makes the point, "...the husband in all his conversation (course of manners and behaviors) with the wife should manifest the same spirit which the Lord Jesus did toward the church."

   <u>*"...even as Christ loved the church..."*</u>
   The love which Christ has for the church is the greatest love the world has ever evidenced. Likewise, a husband is in no danger of loving his wife too much. A man that loves God most will love his wife well. Make the love which Christ had for the church your model as a husband.

   <u>...and gave himself for it...</u>
   Jesus Christ gave himself to die that we might be redeemed and have eternal life. A wife has a biblical expectation

that her husband will deny himself and give himself to promote her happiness and security. That he will support her and provide for her needs spiritually, emotionally and physically. That he will keep her safe from harm and attend to her sickness. She has a biblical expectation that through his love for her he will give himself for her.

2) A woman has a biblical expectation to be respected by her husband as he learns to dwell with her according to knowledge of her. Women differ from each other far more than men do, so the only way a man can gain knowledge of his wife which God requires of him is through conversations with her.

Likewise, ye husbands, dwell with them according to knowledge, giving honour unto the wife, as unto the weaker vessel, and as being heirs together of the grace of life; that your prayers be not hindered. (1st Peter 3:7)

...dwell with them according to knowledge...

Mr. Webster sheds light on what Paul is telling husbands by giving us this definition of the word knowledge, "A clear and certain perception... of truth and fact; the perception of the connection and agreement."

A man lives with his wife according to the knowledge he has of her needs within the agreement of marriage thus it is important that the husband know what his wife's biblical needs are and what her personal preferences are it is important that a husband seek to know, anticipate and fulfill his wife's needs.

...giving honour unto the wife...
Honor goes deeper than respect. For a man to honor his wife he must express that he values her by treating her respectfully in word, in deed, by his behaviors toward her, in honesty and in providing for her spiritual, emotional and physical needs. A woman has a biblical expectation to be respected and honored by her husband.

3) A woman has a biblical expectation for her husband to bear her burdens.
...dwell with them according to knowledge,... as unto the weaker vessel... (1st Peter 3:7)
A loving and caring husband will help bear his wife's burdens spiritually, emotionally and physically. This includes helping with household chores such as laundry,

vacuuming, and doing the dishes, this is especially needed when both spouses work outside of the home. It is also important to make certain home repairs are done when needed. And assisting with the children when they come into the marriage. A man that is helping his wife with her burdens will strengthen his bond with her. Serving is an outward expression of inward love.

4) A woman has a biblical expectation to be led spiritually by her husband.
23) For the husband is the head of the wife, even as Christ is the head of the church: and he is the saviour of the body. 24) Therefore as the church is subject unto Christ, so let the wives be to their own husbands in every thing. (Ephesians 5:23-24)

> *"...the husband is the head of the wife..."*
> The word *"head"* is the idea of being the principal person or the leader. God appointed the man to lead his wife and especially in spiritual matters. Verse 23 continues, *"...even as Christ is the head of the church and he is the savior of the body."*
> A husband does not have the power to redeem his wife's soul from eternal damnation, but he does have a

responsibility to make certain she knows Christ as her own personal Saviour. He has a responsibility to lead her spiritually and a wife has an expectation to be led spiritually by her husband. In order for a man to lead his wife spiritually he must first follow Christ faithfully.

The Lord Jesus teaches us that the husband should lead his wife by serving her. Servant leadership works only on those who are willing to be led. In Mark 10:42-44 Jesus teaches, *42) ...Ye know that they which are accounted to rule over the Gentiles exercise lordship over them; and their great ones exercise authority upon them. 43) But so shall it not be among you: but whosoever will be great among you, shall be your minister: 44) And whosoever of you will be the chiefest, shall be servant of all.*

5) Financial Stability: A woman has a biblical expectation of her, and her children being provided for. *But if any provide not for his own, and specially for those of his own house, he hath denied the faith, and is worse than an infidel.* (1st Timothy 5:8)

Another verse of scripture that reinforces this point is Genesis 24:67 *And Isaac brought her into his mother Sarah's tent,*

*and took Rebekah, and she became his wife;
and he loved her: and Isaac was comforted
after his mother's death.* In this verse we
see that Issac provided the tent. This
teaches that a man's offer to his bride
should include food, clothing, and shelter.
A man must convince his wife that he loves
her for her to be able to comfort him as God
desires.

Financial stability is very important to a
woman and to a young bride's parents.
Sometimes financial resources are limited
and unexpected expenditures arise. Most
women will understand this; however, it is
important that the husband be a good
steward of the resources he has including
his ability to earn money. He needs to be
willing to work an extra job if necessary,
cut back on unnecessary expenditures and
strive to provide for his wife and family's
physical and financial needs. A woman
needs stability in this area and has a
biblical expectation of being provided for.

6) A woman has a biblical expectation of
   receiving affection from her husband.
   *Let the husband render unto the wife due
   benevolence: and likewise also the wife unto
   the husband.* (1st Corinthians 7:3)

The word benevolence means, "kindness, charitableness, love… accompanied with a desire to promote happiness."

Benevolence or affection is expressed in many ways. A man can express affection to his wife by having a date night, by spending time away with her alone to get away from the monotony of life. By spoken words and by words not spoken verbally. By soft physical touch, by being in a crowded room and whispering softly to her, "I love you". By listening carefully to her needs, wants, desires and dreams.

7) A woman has a biblical expectation of her husband being trustworthy.
"The heart of her husband doth safely trust in her…" (Proverbs 31:11)

It would not be just for a man to trust his wife if his wife is unable to trust him. Trust is the most important component in any relationship, but it is a cornerstone to the foundation of a good marriage. Trust is defined as, "confidence, reliance or resting of the mind in the integrity, veracity, justice, friendship, or other sound principle of another person.".

A man must be open and honest with his wife about finances, activities, and personal struggles. A woman will not follow a man or willingly give herself to him if she cannot trust him to be open and honest with her.

The most important element of establishing trust is for him to protect her purity from his passions and from hers until after they marry.

8) A Woman has a Biblical Expectation of her viewpoint being considered.

An important way a wife can help her husband is by explaining her perspective. Women think differently from men, so the challenge is the husband understanding the benefits of his wife's overall awareness of the situation, particularly when children are involved.

God created women to be a suitable help for their husbands. A woman has a built-in drive to find happiness in having her husband appreciate her views, and experience shows that her perspective often helps him carry out his goals. Men should consider the old wise saying, "Behind every successful man, is a woman with a good intuition." (Paraphrased)

I understand that it was necessary for Jesus to go to the Cross for our redemption. However, Pilate could have benefited from taking heed of his wife's intuition. Matthew 27:19 says, *"When he was set down on the judgment seat, his wife sent unto him, saying, Have thou nothing to do with that just man: for I have suffered many things this day in a dream because of him."*

A wise husband will value and consider his wife's viewpoint. God gave her to him to be a help and blessing to him. A wife knows her husband, she knows his thinking process, she sees things he cannot see. Her spiritual gift is different, and her perspective is different.

I speak from experience, there were times my wife tried to give me her perspective on a decision or situation, but I let my pride interfere and did not listen to her wisdom. Many of the times I ignored her counsel and female intuition, things did not work out well. A wise husband will listen to his wife's perspective.

9) A woman has a biblical expectation to be praised by her husband.
Her children arise up, and call her blessed; her husband also, and he praiseth her.
(Proverbs 31:28)

Reading Proverbs 31:10-27 we find the attributes of a virtuous woman. (Before reading further I encourage you to read Proverbs 31:10-27 first) We could ask the question, "Does the husband praise the wife because she is virtuous?" Or "Is the woman virtuous because her husband praises her?" I suggest the answer to both questions is, Yes!

A man should never speak ill of his wife to others, On the contrary, he should praise her both in public and in private. By praising her he expresses his trust, his affection, and appreciation to her as his wife.

The wise husband will seek to live up to the biblical expectations of his wife!

Expectations in Marriage
Part Two

For Ladies

Biblical Expectations for the Wife in Marriage

Just as scripture outlines the husband's responsibilities to his wife, they also tell us what the husband can expect from his wife in the marriage relationship.

Ladies, as you read through this list keep in mind that each topic is a biblical expectation a man has of his wife.

1) A Man has a Biblical expectation for his wife to be a help who is suitable for him, to respect him, to honor him and submit to him when she would rather do something else.
    "And the Lord God said, It is not good that the man should be alone; I will make him an help meet for him." (Genesis 2:18)
    A wife is most helpful to her husband when she sees that being a wife to him is God's calling on her life.

    What did God have in mind when He said, *I will make an help-meet for him.*?

According to Biblical scholar Dr. David Noel Freedman the word *help* is from a word with a combination of two roots, one meaning "to rescue, to save" and the other meaning "to be strong". Mr. Webster says the word *meet* means "suitable as to a use or purpose." Others have defined the word "help" as, "one who does what the man cannot do for himself."

How can a wife be a suitable help to her husband? The old saying is, "Behind every successful man there is a woman". More importantly, behind the successful man is a supportive woman. A woman that cheers for her husband and is always whispering words of confidence into his spirit. A *helpmeet* cheers for her husband and focuses on his strengths not his weaknesses. She does not tear him down but seeks to build him up. She believes in his potential and expresses her belief in him to others.

Nowhere in scripture do we find a man ever criticizing his wife and only twice do we find a wife who criticized her husband. Abigail criticized Nabal the day after he sobered up from an embarrassing night of drunkenness. (1st

Samuel 25:36-38) She did not make a scene or criticize him publicly. She waited until the next day after he had sobered up and talked to him privately. Sometimes constructive criticism is necessary and when necessary should always be constructive and done in private.

The second time we find a wife criticizing her husband is when David's wife Michal criticized him for dancing in the street. (2nd Samuel 6:14-23) Verse sixteen says she, ...*despised him in her heart.* Michal criticized David harshly for doing what he believed the Lord wanted him to do. Her criticism was not constructive and from that day forward David avoided her.

A wife's confidence in her husband and her expression of that confidence is very important to him. Her opinion of him is more important than anyone else's. A wife is extremely helpful to her husband when she praises him and focuses on his strengths. Men don't like to admit it, but a man who love a woman can be hurt deeply by her criticism. And his confidence can be strengthened deeply by her praise.

2) A man has a biblical expectation for his wife to provide companionship.

It is not good that the man should be alone. (Genesis 2:18)

A companion is the opposite of an adversary. In Malachi 2:14 the Prophet refers to the wife as the husband's *companion*. God has called the wife to come along the side of her husband, to keep company with him, to be his friend and confidant. It is important that a woman seek ways to bond with her husband spiritually, emotionally, verbally, and physically, which includes physical intimacy.

Continual bonding is the knitting of two hearts together in the marriage relationship will help the marriage continually grow stronger, but men and women bond differently. Women bone by telling each other about their feelings. Men bond by doing things together.

3) A Man has a biblical expectation of his wife being submissive and obedient while being supportive.

"Wives, submit yourselves unto your own husbands, as unto the Lord." (Ephesians 5:22)

I think men and women miss the spiritual significance of Paul's words in

Ephesians 5:22. First, let me point out what it does **not** mean. It does **not** mean that a husband is to verbally or physically abuse his wife it does not mean he's supposed to use her as a doormat. The word *submit* means to "yield, resign, or surrender to the person, will or authority of another, with the reciprocal pronoun". Having been created in the image of God along with her husband, it would not be robbery for a wife to think herself to be equal with him, but God does expect her to take on the attitude of a help meet.

Philippians 2:5-8 says, *"Let this mind be in you, which was also in Christ Jesus:*
6) Who, being in the form of God, thought it not robbery to be equal with God:
7) But made himself of no reputation, and took upon him the form of a servant, and was made in the likeness of men:
8) And being found in fashion as a man, he humbled himself, and became obedient unto death, even the death of the cross."

Consider the statement, "*as unto the Lord.*" This is the idea of the wife serving God by submitting to her husband and seeing being a wife to her husband as God's calling on her life.

Secondly, Paul says in Ephesians 5:21, *"Submitting yourselves one to another..."*

This explains that the husband and wife are to yield to one another. Jesus told His people to lead by serving. A man serves God by serving his wife, she serves God by serving her husband because that is what God wants from each of them.

However, there is only one head in the family, and God ordained that to be the husband. When a wife submits to her husband she follows his leadership in the home. Biblical submission in marriage brings harmony to the marriage relationship and strengthens the husband's bond to his wife. A man has a biblical expectation of his wife being submissive to him.

4) A man has the biblical expectation of his wife being respectful to him.
   "Nevertheless let every one of you in particular so love his wife even as himself; and the wife see that she reverence her husband." (Ephesians 5:33)
   The word _reverence_ means, "fear mingled with respect, esteem... and affection." A wife should respect her husband's biblical position as head of the family. Having respect and valuing her husband's biblical place in her life will cause her to follow his decisions, speak

respectfully to him in public and encourage him in private. When the wife disagrees with her husband on any issue she can do so in a respectful manner.

He needs confidence that she will honor him in spite of his mistakes. If he lacks that, he will try to cover up his mistakes and weaknesses such that she can't help him effectively.

5) A man has a biblical expectation for his wife to be a keeper at home.

In the Apostle Paul's letter to Titus, he advises him to instruct the older women to teach the young women, *"To be discreet, chaste, keepers at home, good, obedient to their own husbands, that the word of God be not blasphemed."* (Titus 2:5)

A keeper is "One who has the care, custody or superintendence of anything". The care and management of the home can be a challenge for a wife that works outside of the home, and when this is the case the husband should assist his wife with the household chores. However, the scriptures tells us that the care of the home is the primary responsibility of the wife.

A virtuous wife should make keeping a clean and well managed home for her husband a priority in her marriage.

6) A man has a biblical expectation for his wife to meet his physical need of a sexual relationship.

Our focus in this book is on marrying the right one. Therefore, we will not discuss the details of the physical intimacy of the marriage relationship here. Except to say that a woman needs to understand a man has physical desires that are her biblical responsibility to meet. And thus, she should spiritually, emotionally, and physically prepare herself for meeting them before her wedding night.

I suggest young couples purchase and read the book The Act of Marriage by Tim and Beverly LaHaye approximately one week before their wedding. I recommend they both have separate copies and read the book separately prior to marriage and then read the book together after marriage.

In-Laws and Out-Laws

We love our parents but when it comes to marriage parents can be a blessing or a burden to a couple starting out. In Scripture we find examples of good in laws and bad in laws. David's father-in-law tried to kill him. Naomi was such a good mother-in-law to Ruth that Ruth abandoned her own family and moved to Israel to follow the Lord. Moses father-in-law Jethro gave him good advice and was supportive of him.

When a couple enters marriage it is a blessing to have supportive parents on both sides. If you have supportive parents be thankful for that. The following are suggestions based on biblical principles concerning marriage and in laws.

These principles are not necessarily based on whether or not you have supportive parents and will have supportive in laws or not. These principles are based on biblical truths.

Leave and Cleave

Adam makes a profound statement when he wakes up from having a rib removed and sees his wife for the first time. Genesis 2:23-24 And Adam said, *"This is now bone of my bones, and flesh of my flesh: she shall be called Woman, because she was taken out of Man. 24) Therefore shall a man leave his father and his mother, and shall cleave unto his wife: and they shall be one flesh."*

When a man marries a wife he should leave his parents, to leave means "to withdraw or depart from." To cleave means "to unite or be united closely in interest or affection to adhere, to be joined with strong attachment." What does this mean for the young person planning for marriage and what does this mean to the newly married couple?

A young couple entering marriage needs to understand that the only way two individuals can become "one flesh" spiritually, emotionally, and physically is to die to their former individual lives, give up their individual goals, and make a new commitment to serving one another and to serving the new family they are vowing to create.

A married couple must focus on each other and their marriage relationship. This becomes a challenge if their parents interfere. There must be understanding on both sides. The newlyweds need to be understanding of the idea that it is not easy for parents to "let go" of their children even in marriage. And the parents need to understand that they actually brought their child up for the purpose of one day finding a spouse. This is the reason that in the weddings I have conducted over the years I made this point during the wedding rehearsal period I always point out the significance of the question "Who gives this woman to be married to this man?."

This symbolizes the leave and cleave principle. In marriage the man leaves his family to cleave to and care for his wife. Protecting her and caring for her becomes his responsibility. This is no longer the responsibility of her father or mother. In the wedding ceremony he vows to love, honor, keep in sickness and in health and forsake all others for the woman he is marrying. Her parents give her to him with the expectation that he will keep his vows.

However, scripture does not tell the woman to leave her parents and cleave to her husband. Why is this? We are reminded that the woman is instructed to *"...submit yourselves unto your own husbands, as unto the Lord."* (Ephesians 5:22) We addressed this in Expectations Part Two. I quote from that chapter, "When a wife submits to her husband she follows his leadership in the home. Biblical submission in marriage brings harmony to the marriage relationship and strengthens the husband's bond to his wife." Jesus made it clear that he expects his people to lead by serving. That is why we say that the husband and wife must both give up their own goals in favor of serving each other. Servant leadership works only for those who's willing to follow. That's why women should choose to put on the meek and quiet spirit and choose to follow their husbands.

A man needs to understand that his wife's family has been her emotional support for all her life and her parents have been her financial support for most if not all of her life. If a man does not meet these needs his wife will look to her family for support.

Another area of importance is when children come into the family, the wife will need the support she grew up with. It is usually the woman's mother that comes to assist with the baby and sometimes the father's mother will come by as well. Any other woman understands the needs of a new mother far more than a husband will ever understand.

Set Boundaries

A newly married couple must create their own traditions and customs while participating in the traditions and customs of both families. As difficult as it may be for some family members the newlyweds must set boundaries and agree on them.

Sadly, some in laws can push themselves too far into their married adult child's life and interfere in the marriage, when this is evident the parent must understand, "We (spouse and I) have decided we are going to do this in this manner. We love you but this is what we believe is best for us." You must be loving, be respectful *("Honor thy Father and thy Mother")*, but if the parents push, you must be firm.

Holidays

It is important to agree on how you will spend your holidays before you are married and be prepared to change your plans as reality directs. Be considerate and understanding in this area it is wise to be respectful of your spouse's special holiday family traditions it's also important to make your own holiday traditions.

Relationship Behaviors

Growing up in our families we learn relationship behaviors from our early life role models. We also develop habits and preferences that may differ from our spouses when we get married. And your spouse will have learned relationship behaviors and have developed habits, and preferences that differ from ours. Most newlyweds can work through the differences because they are in love and focused on one another. However, the in-laws may question your preference in any given area.

Everyone is different, so be respectful, understanding, and considerate.

Baggage

I use the term "baggage" to cover an array of topics including, trauma, anger, jealousy, bitterness, destructive relationships behaviors and past romantic relationships that had a negative effect. Because we are not having a personal conversation about the baggage that your bride or groom might bring into your marriage I must speak in generalities. The following are some principles to follow if and when you have to deal with baggage in your marriage.

Address the baggage before your marriage if possible.

The truth is the "baggage" is usually overlooked or not revealed before marriage because we are focused on the strengths of our intended spouse and when we do see a blemish we tend to ignore it. The challenge is that after marriage the "baggage" will begin to unpack itself. It is best to deal with any issues as soon as possible. So, if you don't see it before the wedding, deal with it as soon as it comes to light.

Be understanding.

Once you are married and living in the same home you will find small things about your spouse that you don't like. This is normal for most newlyweds, be understanding and reasonable, you will have baggage that your spouse won't like either.

Discuss these things as they come up and *"reason together"* and work through them.

<u>Unpacking the big suitcases</u>
Sometimes two people come together in marriage with one or both of them having a large piece of baggage. This baggage could have been packed in a variety of ways and with a variety of behaviors and issues. Sometimes this suitcase was packed by parents. I've learned that good relationship behaviors and first taught in the home and so are bad ones. If a person is reared in a home of bitterness, wrath, anger, malice, evil speaking, and turmoil, they will likely carry the baggage into their marriage. These things cause trauma and emotional issues. When the baggage is big the effects on the marriage relationship will also be big.

This baggage must be unpacked carefully. If this is something you find yourself dealing with before or after your marriage you must deal with it immediately, biblically, prayerfully and carefully. My first suggestion is talk to your pastor. If he cannot help for whatever reason, find a Bible based counselor that can help you. Don't lose the person you love for something God can give you victory over.

If You Find Yourself in a Bad Situation

What if you marry the person you love, but your in-laws are lost, unbelievers, or even outright reject everything you believe? What if they reject you and your marriage? What can you do?

Unfortunately, this does happen, and it is difficult to endure. I don't have all the answers, but I offer these suggestions:

Love Your Spouse

Let your unconditional love of your spouse be a testimony to your in-laws or your parents, however the case may be. If you believe God has given your spouse to you and you know that they are the one, let the behaviors of your love speak for you.

Don't allow the In-laws and Out-laws to come between you and your spouse.

Criticizing your spouse's parents to your spouse would be an example of allowing your In-laws to come between you and your spouse. Keep in mind that you married your spouse, not their parents; even though they came with the package, they are not the package.

Speaking ill of them and criticizing them will not help your marriage relationship.

Ask Your In-laws for Advice

You may find this suggestion a little strange, but it can soften their heart. Ask them for advice about a matter that you know what kind of advice they will give you, something that is not controversial. Ask for advice about something that is a strength for them. For example, if you are considering a specific purchase, ask them where they think you should shop for the item. Or if you are taking a trip to an unfamiliar area, ask them which route they think would be best and if they know anything about the area.

Asking them for advice expresses that you value them and will make them feel needed. Be sure to thank them and later tell them the advice was helpful.

Stand Your Ground Respectfully

You don't have to accept verbal abuse and don't allow any family member to abuse your spouse verbally. I learned long ago that there are some people you must love from a distance, including family members. You can be firm; you can be strong, and you can do so respectfully and lovingly. Speak the truth in love!

Pray

Prayer will do wonders! Prayer is the best weapon against those who see us as an enemy.

Ask God to work in their heart, ask Him to help them with whatever issues they may have, and pray that you do not become bitter but that you always respond in a Christ-like manner.

People are People

We are all different, yet we are the same. We have different needs, likes, dislikes and preferences. Yet we have the basic human needs to be loved, to feel important, to have hope and purpose for our lives. It is important that a husband makes his wife feel safe, this includes feeling safe from the In-laws and Out-laws. Be respectful to all concerned, but above all your spouse will be the second most important person in your life, second to God. Focus on HIM and your spouse.

Thoughts on the Song of Solomon

By
[1]Bill and Roberta Taylor

The Song of Songs is a poem which was written in Hebrew three or four thousand years ago to explain how husbands and wives should interact.

It was preserved by meticulous hand-copying over the centuries because it so well captures the principles of maintaining a happy marriage.

It starts with the wife praising her husband, right at the beginning. This works because just about every man has strong physical desires. Feeling appreciated by his wife makes a man more inclined to take care of her and to appreciate her by praising her in return.

There is no criticism AT ALL in the Song of Solomon, only praise in mind-numbing detail. The man and wife are constantly looking for little things about each other to praise and appreciate. The way it's worded sounds odd to us, but you can easily re-word it to make sense in modern terms. The main thing to learn is that married people

---

[1] Bill Taylor, Evangelist of the Printed Word
successful-marriage.blogspot.com

need constant praise, support, and affirmation from each other.

The husband is totally involved with his wife. He tells everyone that he believes she's uniquely perfect:

Song of Solomon 6:9 *"My dove, my undefiled is but one; she is the only one of her mother, she is the choice one of her that bare her. The daughters saw her, and blessed her; yea, the queens and the concubines, and they praised her."*

He's so focused on her that he doesn't see other women as women, only as people. The wife has the security of knowing that her husband belongs to her: Song of Solomon 2:16, *"My beloved is mine, and I am his: he feedeth among the lilies."*

Song of Solomon 6:3, *"I am my beloved's, and my beloved is mine: he feedeth among the lilies."*

How should a man behave to convince his wife that he belongs to her?

The wife recognizes and encourages her husband's desire for her: Song of Solomon 7:10, *"I am my beloved's, and his desire is toward me."*

The specific way she encourages him to keep his desire focused on her as opposed to all those other women out there is explained in the next few verses. It also convinces him that she belongs to him.

Reading through the Song of Solomon we find that the wife asks her mother for advice. The bottom line is that the wife has the responsibility to meet her husband's physical desires for intimacy. Denying his desires will push him away and can cause him to be tempted by other women.

The entire Song deals with her need to be appreciated. A man can't praise his wife in such detail without paying close attention. Marriages are based on communication; a woman communicates heart-to-heart; a man communicates with physical intimacy.

How many marriages would fail if husband and wife never, not ever, criticized each other and appreciated each other instead? That is the essence of the Song of Solomon.

I encourage engaged couples to read the Song of Solomon individually two weeks before their wedding and then read it together after their wedding.

Thirty Pieces of Silver

Judas sold Jesus for thirty pieces of silver, ...*And they took the thirty pieces of silver, the price of him that was valued, whom they of the children of Israel did value;* (Matthew 27:9) The Chief Priests set the value of Jesus at thirty pieces of silver. You and I would agree that Jesus is much more valuable to us than a mere thirty pieces of silver. I'm sure you would agree that we are unable to determine the value of Jesus Christ or what He has done for mankind.

Not only is Jesus more valuable to us than thirty pieces of silver, but we are more valuable to Him than thirty pieces of silver. Jesus determined our value to be equal or more than His own life. He valued you and I so much that He shed His innocent blood for our eternal souls. He valued our lives and our souls worthy of His own life. Selah! Take a moment and think about that, think about how valuable you are to God.

In our closet relationships, marriage, family, and friendships we want to be valued! May I also suggest that in all of those relationships we should also seek to be valuable.

Paul tells us we should value one another, Philippians 2:3 *"Let nothing be done through strife or vainglory; but in lowliness of mind let each esteem other better than themselves."* The principle of being valued and being valuable is extremely important in the marriage relationship.

How to express value during courtship that will follow us into our marriage?

Show Respect

We see this principle in Philippians 3:2 mentioned above. The Apostle Paul also instructs us about respecting one another in marriage, In Ephesians 5:28 and 33, *28) "So ought men to love their wives as their own bodies. He that loveth his wife loveth himself." 33) "Nevertheless let every one of you in particular so love his wife even as himself; and the wife see that she reverence her husband."*

Mr. Webster give a list of definitions to what Respect is, I believe the following best describes what Paul is telling us; "To view or consider with some degree of reverence; to esteem as possessed of real worth." Shared respect for one another flows from mutually valuing one another and being valuable to one another.

Speaking kindly expresses value

Ephesians 4:29 tells us, *"Let no corrupt (destructive) communication proceed out of your mouth, but that which is good (kind, good will) to*

74

the use of edifying (Building up in knowledge), that it may minister grace unto the hearers." The most practical way to express value to anyone is simply through verbal communication. Through the tone and the words, we speak to them we can strengthen their confidence, encourage them and give them assurance that they are valued.

My friends Bill and Roberta Taylor have been studying marriage for fifty years, they teach the "Only Praise" principle. Speak words of praise as often as possible, always seek to build up, and never tear down. Focus on strengths not weaknesses.

Responding softly expresses value
Proverbs 15:1 says, *"A soft answer turneth away wrath (the effects of anger); but grievous (afflictive, painful) words stir up anger."* Anyone with a serious anger problem is going to find this difficult. If we have anger in our heart toward a loved one we must figure out why the emotion of anger is there and deal with the issue. Resolving an ager problem is an important manner of expressing value.

Listening expresses Value
Someone wisely said, "The biggest communication problem is, we do not listen to understand. We listen to reply". When you truly listen to someone you experience the whole person, not only what they are saying, but why

they are saying it, and who they are. Listening is a very important way of expressing value.

Investing time expresses value

Perspective is important, for example we should see time with our loved ones as time invested not time spent. Courtship is an important investment of time for a couple to get acquainted with one another and as they get closer to their wedding day it is a time to listen to each other and learn about each other as well as a time to discuss their future together.

Improving myself expresses value to my loved ones

When we make our own spiritual growth a priority in our lives we express to our loved ones that we value them, that we want to be the best "us" we can be for them.

Making Ourselves Valuable During Courtship that Will Follow us into Marriage.

We have made six suggestions about the importance of valuing our intended spouse, now we look at the other side of the proverbial coin, being valuable, or making ourselves valuable.

Be respectable

Be a person of character, keep your word, express gratitude, continually work on your own spiritual growth. Be clean spiritually, emotionally and physically.

Speaking kindly expresses value, but it also makes you valuable, be the one that communicates edification, confidence, courage and praise.

Responding softly makes you valuable
Be the one that responds with patience, understanding, forgiveness and love.

Being a good listener makes you valuable
Be the one that listens to understand and experiences the whole person. Being a good listener makes you very valuable.

Making it a priority to invest your time in a relationship makes you valuable
Be the one willing to invest your time in the relationship and in the person. Be the one that makes good use of time invested in conversations to get to know the other person, their needs, their desires and their dreams.

Improving yourself makes you valuable
Be the one that seeks to make yourself more valuable by improving yourself, your relationship skills. Spiritual growth does not happen by accident, it happens on purpose. Learn to be a good listener, an encourager, a builder of confidence, an encourager, a friend and a lover. Make yourself valuable to the people that are most valuable to you in life.

Important Questions to Ask Yourself About Choosing a Spouse

Whoso findeth a wife findeth a good thing, and obtaineth favour of the LORD. (Proverbs 18:22)

Therefore shall a man leave his father and his mother, and shall cleave unto his wife: and they shall be one flesh. (Genesis 2:24)

Have ye not read, that he which made them at the beginning made them male and female, And said, For this cause shall a man leave father and mother, and shall cleave to his wife: and they twain shall be one flesh? Wherefore they are no more twain, but one flesh. What therefore God hath joined together, let not man put asunder. (Matthew 19:4–6)

Deciding whom you will marry is the second most important decision you will ever make in life, second only to your salvation. Before entering a relationship that could develop into a romantic relationship and then lead to marriage, you must ask yourself some important questions. The purposes of asking these questions are many: to help you avoid heartache, choose the right one, choose the right reasons and choose the right circumstances. My prayer is that the following questions will help you in choosing the spouse who will bring you true love, joy and happiness for the rest of your life.

What Is My Ideal Spouse?

"Who can find a virtuous woman? for her price is far above rubies." (Proverbs 31:10)

As we consider our first question, I think of the words in Proverbs 31:10 which ask, *"Who can find a virtuous woman?"* Of course, I realize that if you are a young woman you would ask, "Who can find a virtuous man?" Perhaps "virtuous" describes the key ingredient you should look for in the person whom you choose to be your spouse. Webster's Dictionary 1828 of the English Language defines "virtuous" as "morally good; acting in conformity to the moral law; practicing the moral duties and abstaining from vice; chaste." [2]Mrs. Cathy Rice, widow of [3]Dr. Bill Rice, shares an interesting story in her book. She tells how she determined what to look for in a husband.

---

[2] The Right Romance in Marriage was first published by the Sword of the Lord Publishers in 1966.
[3] Dr. Bill Rice, 1912–1978. Greatly used evangelist, founder of the Bill Rice Ranch in Murfreesboro, Tennessee, the world's largest ministry to the deaf.

"I probably thought more seriously about marriage than most girls. My father and mother were and still are happily married, but so many of my girlfriends' parents were not. Why? I often wondered about this. As I sat pondering the question one day, the thought came to me that a girl certainly needed to pray about her marriage and then have enough patience to wait until the right man came along. But how would I know the right man?

That day I wrote down what I would expect to find in my ideal man. I have kept that list to this day, and I share it with you now.

My Ideal Man

In searching for my lover and mate, I look for the following characteristics in him:

1. He MUST be a Christian.

2. He MUST be truthful.

3. He must be stable, standing on his own feet with plenty of hard, solid backbone and a mind of his own.

4. He must be brave; never a coward, cheat, sneak or one to mind the other fellow's business; never a bully to run over the weak and small but always ready to help those less fortunate than he.

5. He must be a good sport.

6. He must not be idle, spending time loafing about poolrooms, drugstores, etc., but be a man who finds useful ways of spending all his time.

7. He must be a leader among men. By this I mean one who can make his influence felt; not one that always follows.

8. He must have a high regard for women above all, his sweetheart and wife.

9. He must have ambition.

10. He must have an appreciation for good music, art and literature.

11. He must not be a fanatic on any one subject.

12. He must not use profane language or have a temper he is unable to control.

13. He must not drink or smoke.

14. He must be a man, not a sissy.

15. He must be nice looking, neat and tidy in dress, clean inside and out.

16. He must be able to understand me in all my ways.

17. He must be dependable; one that I can put all my faith, trust and confidence in; one I will be happy to confide in.

18. He must have faith, trust and confidence in me and be willing and glad to confide in me and will let me share all his trials and troubles.

19. He must be a man that will let me be his dearest friend, chum and pal on earth; who will let me walk hand in hand with him to his goal.

20. He must love me with all his heart and soul and receive the same love from me in return."

(Signed) Mary Catherine Widner, 1933

As I read this now, I realize I had my sights high. But when I met Bill and we had been friends for a while, one day I read the above and said to myself, You know what? I believe he fits everything on that list. And today, after thirty wonderful years together, he fits it even more. How good it is to be in love with my ideal man."

` ` ` ` ` ` ` ` ` ` ` ` ` ` ` ` ` ` ` ` ` ` ` ` ` ` ` ` ` ` ` ` ` ` ` `

Have you determined what your ideal spouse is? I suggest that you take some time after you finish reading this book and do as Mrs. Cathy Rice did. Write down what you believe would be your ideal man or woman. And use that as your standard, asking the Lord to lead you to that person.

Is This Person a Believer in Jesus Christ?

"Be ye not unequally yoked together with unbelievers: for what fellowship hath righteousness with unrighteousness? and what communion hath light with darkness? And what concord hath Christ with Belial [wickedness]? or what part hath he that believeth with an infidel [unbeliever]? And what agreement hath the temple of God with idols? for ye are the temple of the living God; as God hath said, I will dwell in them, and walk in them; and I will be their God, and they shall be my people."
2nd Corinthians 6:14–16

"Can two walk together, except they be agreed?"
Amos 3:3.

The number one priority in choosing a spouse is that you choose one who is a Christian. You must first be sure of your salvation. Then, when looking for a spouse, you choose one that is a Christian. Make it a priority to discuss it and make sure that he or she believes in the Lord Jesus Christ and has received Him as his or her personal Saviour.

A nonbeliever will not share your priorities, and you cannot have a proper emotional-spiritual relationship with a nonbeliever. Dr. Lester Roloff said, "If you marry an unsaved person, you will have the Devil as a daddy-in-law." A person who does not have the Holy Spirit dwelling in him will not have the same desires you have, the same outlook on life that you have or the same type of emotions you have, because he does not have the same spiritual Father that you have.

Then we must consider a very harsh reality: why spend your life with someone that you will spend eternity without? You may think, I am interested in a nonbeliever, but I am going to win him to the Lord; I am going to make a Christian out of him. Well, that all sounds good, but the truth is, a nonbeliever will be more likely to pull you down than you will be to pull him up. It is always easier to knock someone off a ladder than it is to pull him or her up the ladder. You will find the same to be true spiritually. It is easier for you to be pulled down than for you to pull someone up. It is best if the person you have an interest in is already a believer.

Let's take this point to the next level. Not only should you choose a person who is a believer, but it is best if he or she is of the same faith you hold. It is best if she or he has the same Christian philosophy you have.

Any wrong relationship with a nonbeliever will grieve and quench the Holy Spirit.

Is There Spiritual Fruit in This Person's Life?

"But the fruit of the Spirit is love, joy, peace, long suffering, gentleness, goodness, faith, Meekness, temperance: against such there is no law. And they

that are Christ's have crucified the flesh with the affections and lusts. If we live in the Sprit, let us also walk in the Spirit. Let us not be desirous [coveting] of vain glory, provoking one another, envying one another" (Galatians 5:22–26)

It is one thing for a person to say he is a Christian, but it another thing for a person to be a genuine believer in Jesus Christ. The evidence is in the fruit he bears in his life.

A lot of people can talk the Christian talk but are unable to walk the walk. A person who is truly born again and has the Holy Spirit of God dwelling in him will bear the fruit of the Spirit.

When someone is seeking a spouse, it is wise to observe whether or not there is Christlike behavior in the life of the person being considered. Does he have a genuine concern and interest in the things of God?

Does he exhibit Christian character? Does he have a daily personal walk with God through prayer and Bible study? Does he have a desire to share Christ with others? Is he selfish or concerned for others? Is he grounded in a good, Bible-believing church, and is he faithful to the services and ministries of that church?

Let's consider the fruits of the Spirit as described in Galatians, chapter 5, and use them as our standard.

The Fruit of Love:
Love is an action word; love gives. Selfishness and lust always take, but love seeks to give. Love focuses on the object of affection; lust focuses on self.

The Fruit of Joy:
Joy is what one has on the inside; joy is a positive outlook even in discouraging circumstances. Happiness can be affected by circumstances on the outside, but the joy the Christian can have in his heart through Christ cannot be taken away by those things we cannot control.

The Fruit of Peace:
Peace means being calm, untroubled, set at one again. We Christians can choose the calm, the completeness in our soul that comes through knowing Jesus Christ, or we can allow the flesh to rule us and live with the turmoil of the world.

The Fruit of Longsuffering (Patience):
Longsuffering describes one who is not hasty to retaliate, but who suffers long, bears up under burdens, strives patiently toward the goal and seeks to help others along the way.

The Fruit of Gentleness (Kindness):
Gentleness is being useful in helping others.

The Fruit of Goodness:
Goodness refers to beauty or virtue that is on the inside that wants to express itself in deed.

Goodness is a deed committed to help another person, usually without being asked and often anonymously.

The Fruit of Faith:

For the Christian, faith is a dependence upon God, a belief that God is able to meet our needs, a reliance on Him for strength, wisdom and guidance. It means to be faithful to a task, to be faithful to people who depend on us.

The Fruit of Meekness:

Meekness reveals itself in humility, softness of temper, not looking down on others, putting the needs of others before your own needs.

The Fruit of Temperance:

To be temperate is to have self-control. Temperance is probably the one fruit that brings all of the others together. Temperance is being able to control your temper, flesh, desires, attitude, etc.

Is This Relationship the Leading of the Lord?

"Trust in the LORD with all thine heart; and lean not unto thine own understanding. In all thy ways acknowledge him, and he shall direct thy paths" (Proverbs 3: 5-6)

Are you attracted to this person because of his or her appearance, or is the Lord leading you into a relationship? There is nothing wrong with nice looks, and of course one should be clean with good grooming habits and hygiene. However, a spiritual glow within can outshine any skin-deep beauty.

As mentioned earlier, do not seek a relationship for the sake of a relationship. So, you must ask yourself if this is merely a physical attraction. Is this relationship developing because you feel lonely for some companionship, or is this truly the leading of the Lord in your life?

God wants us to have friendships and companions. But enter into a relationship with the leading of the Lord and guard it carefully. In this manner you will develop a lifelong relationship that brings with it devotion, commitment, and responsibilities. Remember, only God knows what tomorrow brings. We cannot predict the future, nor can we see the inner self of a man as God can.

Has This Person Had a Lot of Short-Term "Romantic" Relationships?

And he [Solomon] had seven hundred wives, princesses, and three hundred concubines: and his wives turned away his heart. For it came to pass, when Solomon was old, that his wives turned away his heart after other gods: and his heart was not perfect with the LORD his God, as was the heart of David his father. (1st Kings 11:3-4)

A young man or young lady who goes from romantic relationship to romantic relationship is not only selfish but has some insecurity. It has been my observation that such people are unstable in relationships in other areas of their lives as well. They are usually self-centered and are looking for what they can get out of a relationship instead of what they can give to one.

Granted, such people may have gotten hurt in a relationship in the past, but that does not give them the liberty to take the heart of someone who may care for them just to throw it back as you would a fish after catching it. Numerous short-term relationships may be evidence of an unwillingness to commit, an unwillingness to trust others and a lack of focus on developing a sincere and lasting relationship.

Have I Made Seeking the
Right Person a Serious Matter of Prayer?

Be careful for nothing; but in every thing by prayer and supplication with thanksgiving let your requests be made known unto God. And the peace of God, which passeth all understanding, shall keep your hearts and minds through Christ Jesus. (Philippians 4:6-7)

The word "careful" in our text means to be anxious or troubled about something. I have spoken with many teenagers and young adults who spent too much time worrying about finding a spouse or someone to court when they should have been praying that the Lord would send them the right person.

For the Christian searching for the right person, prayer should be first and foremost. Consider these important things to pray about in finding the right person:

1. Pray about what to put on your personal list of The Ideal Person, as discussed in Question Number One: What Is My Ideal Spouse?

2. Pray and ask the Lord to lead you to the right person and to lead the right person to you.

3. Pray for the right one! After all, it is a priority that you marry the person that the Lord has for you.

4. Pray for the right timing. Do not miss this very important and practical point. You may know the right person as you read this book. He or she may be someone with whom you are already acquainted, but the timing is not right.

I shared this thought with a group of teenagers in a Christian school. I said to them, "The person you are going to marry may be sitting in this auditorium. He or she is the right person for you, the person God has for you, but the timing is not right. You are in the seventh grade, and you have a lot of other things to do before the timing will be right."

My wife and I are certain that we met each other when we were young teenagers. On that day we met only for a few moments. Neither one of us had any idea that we would ever marry. We didn't even know if we would ever meet again, but several years later when we met again in the home of a mutual friend, we both thought in our hearts that we had found the right one.

We began to talk on the phone and then developed a relationship, and now here we are years later, happily married with a wonderful family. The person was right, and the timing was right.

5. Pray for the right circumstances. The person may be right, the timing may be right in that you may be old enough to court or to be married, but are the circumstances right? If you are a sophomore in college with a heavy course load and a lot of financial debt, the circumstances are not right!

6. If you are currently in a relationship that is developing into something romantic, pray for the Lord's will to be done in the relationship.

7. Pray together as a couple. The young man should lead in this but pray together about your relationship each time you are together.

What Kind of Relationship Does This Person Have with His/Her Parents?

Children, obey your parents in the Lord: for this is right. Honour thy father and mother; which is the first commandment with promise; That it may be well with thee, and thou mayest live long on the earth. (Ephesians 6:1–3)

Honor is having the right attitude in obedience. We can conclude that the statement, *"Children, obey your parents,"* is written to dependent children still under the care and provision of their parents. However, whether or not a person was obedient to his parents in his adolescence and teen years says a lot about his character, especially if he was reared in a Christian home. Obedience, respect and general treatment he exhibits toward his parents gives insight into how he will treat others in relationships.

For the older teenager and young adult, the way he honors his parents may be the behavior we should consider. We should do as the Bible instructs us: *"Honor thy father and mother."* I have often told teenagers the Bible does not say honor your mother and father if they are everything you want them to be. There are no stipulations on the command to honor our parents; we are commanded to do it.

To honor is to show respect; respect should be given to parents not because they are good or bad parents, but because they are parents, and the Bible commands it. I will share three principles concerning honoring parents that I have shared with teenagers around the country.

Honor your parents' name

"A good name is rather to be chosen than great riches, and loving favour rather than silver and gold." (Proverbs 22:1)

One of the best ways you can honor your parents is by having a good testimony. Whether or not your parents are Christians, whether or not they are living, we can honor them, their name and in some cases their memory by keeping a good testimony.

Honor your parents in their sunset years by caring for them

It is sad to hear of older people whose children never visit them, call them or check on them. When we are young, we are very dependent on our parents, but when we get older, our parents will become more dependent on us. Christians should be careful to honor their parents as they get older. We should make sure our parents' needs are met—physically, medically and emotionally. Parents of adult children need to know that their children love them.

<u>Honor is having the right attitude in obedience</u>
To obey with complaining and disrespect is dishonor. To honor is to obey with the right attitude. For the young adult, obedience with honor would be to try to fulfill the desires of his parents, provided those desires are biblical and in accordance with the will of God.

The way a person shows honor to his parents and the relationship he has with his parents are important factors to consider when choosing a spouse.

Does the Spiritual Leadership in My Life Approve of This Relationship?

Remember them which have the rule over you, who have spoken unto you the word of God: whose faith follow, considering the end of their conversation.... Obey them that have the rule over you, and submit yourselves: for they watch for your souls, as they that must give account, that they may do it with joy, and not with grief: for that is unprofitable for you. (Hebrews 13:7,17)

I begin with this suggestion: it would be wise first to seek counsel from the spiritual leadership in your life before entering into a courtship. This would make choosing whom to marry go much more smoothly.

Let's examine some statements from our Scripture text. First, consider the phrase,

"Remember them which have the rule over you." The word "remember" as used here means that we are to be mindful of them, the things they have taught us and the investment they have made in our lives.

Second, who are those that *"rule over"* us? I submit that the three most important are our parents, our pastor and those who have taught us the Word of God, such as Sunday school teachers and youth directors, etc. These are the people who watch for our souls and have generally made the largest spiritual investment in our lives through teaching us prayer and love.

Third, observe the statement *"considering the end of their conversation."* The word *"conversation"* used here implies behavior. Webster's Dictionary gives us this definition: "General course of manners; behavior, deportment, especially as it respects morals." In making any important decision in our lives, we should consider the leadership God has put into our lives. We should consider the life example of our leadership— what they have done with their own lives, how God has used them in our lives and how their actions have prospered in the Lord.

Now let's look at our spiritual leadership in a more individual way. We will begin with parents; If you have parents who are born-again believers who love God and are faithful to the Lord, you should listen very closely to their counsel concerning whom you choose to court and whom you choose to marry. Now you may ask if I believe your parents should choose whom you marry. My answer to that question would be NO! I do not think they should choose, but I do believe they should approve, provided they are Christians. I say that because if your parents are not Christians they may have different reasons for wanting you to marry someone else. For example, they may think you should marry a non-Christian for financial or status reasons.

Also, if your parents are not Christians, you should still show them the utmost respect concerning whom you choose to marry. I would also suggest that if you do not have Christian parents, it would be wise to seek the counsel from a good Christian couple who has known you for a long time.

The next spiritual leader to consider in your life is your pastor. Now, I want to be very careful here. Let's say you are in college, and you have a pastor who has been a part of your life for a short amount of time; I think you should seek counsel from this pastor.

However, I also believe it would be wise to seek counsel from the pastor you have had for the longest period of time. For example, it would be wise to seek the counsel of the pastor you had during your teen years because the pastor you have had the longest probably knows you better and has the most invested in your life. You should hold your pastor's counsel in very high regard; he is the man God has sent to you from His heart. *"And I will give you pastors according to mine heart, which shall feed you with knowledge and understanding"* (Jeremiah 3:15)

As I look back on the marriages I have seen over the years, the ones that fared the best are the ones on which good godly pastors put their blessing. Other spiritual leadership in our lives would be our Sunday school teachers, youth directors and their wives, etc.

These are people who have also taught us the Word of God. They have watched for our souls, and they have invested prayer, love and counsel in our lives.

For these reasons, it is important for the spiritual leadership in your life to approve of whom you choose to court and whom you choose to marry: God placed them in your life; they have been down the road you travel; they know more about what is ahead of you than you do; and they know from where you have come.

They have watched for your soul; they have prayed for you, and they have watched you grow spiritually. They know many of your weaknesses and your strengths.

They know God, and they have sought His guidance in leading you.

One final thought: the spiritual leadership in your life should want to meet the person in whom you have an interest and the spiritual leadership in that person's life should want to meet you before giving any definite counsel.

Does the Spiritual Leadership in His / Her Life Approve of This Relationship?

In the previous question we considered the importance of the spiritual leadership in your life. Now we will consider the spiritual leadership in the life of the person you are considering courting and possibly marrying. Because we covered so much in the previous question, we will only consider the aspect of why it is important that the spiritual leaders in your potential spouse's life approve of the relationship.

They know the person's strengths and weaknesses and are aware of any past problems or future potential problems. They know if the timing is right and if the circumstances are right, and because they know these things, they will have a reasonable idea of whether or not you are the right one for him or her.

If you are blessed in having the same pastor and youth leader, you are at an advantage because the spiritual leadership in your life knows both of you and has made an investment in you both. It would be wise to seek counsel from your spiritual leadership individually and together.

Can the Relationship Become a Friendship?

A friend loveth at all times" (Proverbs 17:17) Friendship is the one thing that seems to be the longest lasting in any relationship. True friendship has some wonderful qualities. You can be friends with a brother or sister, a cousin and other relatives; but more importantly, you can be friends with your spouse.

There are people in my life with whom I have been friends for thirty-five years. I have one particular such friend; he lives in Texas now, and I do not get to see him very often, but I do get to talk to him on the phone from time to time, and we always enjoy the fellowship.

Before you become anything else in a relationship become friends. A marriage involves many different relationships. Many young people think the physical intimacy of marriage is the most important aspect. Some think about having children. Some men may think about having someone who will cook for them and take care of their laundry. Some women may think about having a man to protect them and provide for them. Now these things are not particularly wrong, but the most important part of any marriage is friendship. As our Scripture says, *"A friend loveth at all times."* When you are physically unable to care for yourself, let alone a spouse, a true friend will still love you. I want to share a very heart-warming story with you that I believe will make the point of why it is important to let your relationship become a friendship before it becomes a marriage.

My wife's grandparents were married sixty-eight years when God called Grandpa to Heaven; seven months later Grandma followed Grandpa. They were wonderful people. His name was Joe, and her name was Marcella. Grandpa always called her "Marce" for short. A few years before they passed, Grandma had a stroke which led to other medical complications.

Concerns about their health brought the family to terms with placing them into a facility that would be able to care for their needs, a very nice place located in Covington, Kentucky, near where they had lived all of their lives. I used to take my wife and children down to visit them so our children could get to know them. We would remind them that they were still loved and in our thoughts. Grandma's stroke had left her unable to walk, speak, feed herself, dress herself or do much of anything without assistance, so Grandpa took it upon himself to take care of her as much as he could, even in his failing health.

On one particular visit, my wife and I arrived with our children at the assisted living home for a visit with "Great Grandma and Great Grandpa." We checked in at the office as we were required to do before going to the living quarters. At the desk I asked where we would be able to find Joe and Marce. The nurse informed me that they were in the dining room eating lunch. Our family walked down the hall to the dining room entrance. When we got to the door, I observed my wife's precious grandparents sitting at a round table with a lovely white tablecloth decorated with flowers.

They were now in wheelchairs. Grandpa had put an adult-size bib around Grandma's neck, and she was sitting at the table with her head drooped down as was normal since her stroke had left her weak and unable to hold up her head for long periods of time. Grandpa was sitting next to her feeding her with a spoon the way a mother or father would feed a child. The food Grandma was eating would be the equivalent to adult baby food. I took my wife's hand and said, "Let's just wait a moment and watch them." As we stood there, we saw a wonderful portrait of true friendship and of true love. We saw the wedding vows "in sickness and in health" come to life before our eyes.

As we watched, Grandpa would take a spoonful of food and put it on Grandma's lips. He would say, "Come on now, Marce, you can do it; just a few more bites." As she would take the food into her mouth, Grandpa would praise her, "That's good, Marce; you're doing good." Carefully, patiently and lovingly, Grandpa fed the lady who had been his friend for seventy years. When they finished eating, he removed the bib and wiped her chin. Grandpa then maneuvered his wheelchair around so that he could guide Grandma's chair. As he got behind her wheelchair, he would push her forward. Then he would pull his chair up close to hers and push her again. On they went down the hall to their room.

What was Grandpa doing? Why is this important? Before he ever had a physical relationship with her, before he ever romanced her, before they ever discussed marriage, he was her friend. They had always been friends before they were anything else. There they were—she could not speak to him, she could not care for his needs, she could not cook for him, and she could not do the things she had done for so many years.

There was no longer physical intimacy. All of those things were gone, but there was one thing that remained, the thing with which they started out some seventy years before. They were still friends! Joe was just taking care of the best friend he had ever had in his life outside of his Saviour—his precious "Marce"!

There is one more thing Joe was doing that is equally important. Joe kept the promise he had made to Marce sixty-eight years before on June 17, 1926. He promised he would love and cherish her, honor and keep her in sickness as in health, in poverty as in wealth, and forsaking all others, keep only unto her so long as he would live. Until that day on December 18, 1994, when God called for Joe, he took care of his friend Marce. And I might add, until her health failed, Marce took good care of Joe, her best friend.

Before you become anything else in a relationship, become friends.

What Spiritual Goals Does This Person Have?

That I may know him, and the power of his resurrection, and the fellowship of his sufferings, being made conformable unto his death.... I press toward the mark for the prize of the high calling of God in Christ Jesus. (Philippians 3:10,14)

What does your prospective spouse want to do for God? Now I realize that God does not call every man to pastor a church, go to the mission field or become an evangelist. I also realize that not every young lady is going to marry a preacher or be a missionary or missionary's wife, but God does call every Christian to serve Him faithfully. Every believer should have some basic spiritual goals, such as learning the Word of God, having a good prayer life, being a soul winner, having a good testimony and being faithful to the services of his local church.

We should also have more personal and specific goals, things we believe God has for us to do that are special, like being a Sunday school teacher, helping in the church nursery, serving in a nursing home ministry, helping with the maintenance at our church, working in a church bus ministry, serving in a jail ministry or other outreach ministry—simply put, just doing what we can for our Saviour and His cause of reaching souls.

Then there are things we would refer to as spiritual family goals. Such things as purity and having a marriage that honors God, desiring to rear children according to the Bible, having a family altar and having family relationships that honor Christ are other examples of spiritual family goals.

Your goals for the Lord should be influenced and encouraged by your spouse and not hindered. If you do not have similar spiritual goals to aim at, you will be unlikely to reach any of them.

What Life Goals Does This Person Have?

Whatsoever thy hand findeth to do, do it with thy might; for there is no work, nor device, nor knowledge, nor wisdom, in the grave, whither thou goest. (Ecclesiastes 9:10)

"But if any provide not for his own, and specially for those of his own house, he hath denied the faith, and is worse than an infidel." (1st Timothy 5:8)

A young man should pray for a wife whose life goals will encourage what he believes God wants him to do with his life. If he wants to have a family and rear children, it would be important that he prays for a wife that shares those same goals.

May I say that I believe the highest calling for any woman is to be a godly wife and mother! That is not to say a woman cannot work outside of the home; it has just been my humble opinion that it is best that she can stay home and care for the children, if at all possible. For a young lady, it is very important to know what a young man's goals are for his life. I realize that in his early twenties he may not have a clear picture of what he is going to do, but he should have a good idea about it. He should have some ambitions and plans for his future. He should know what his interests are, and he should have an idea of what he is going to do for a living.

I have told young ladies, "If you ask a twenty-year-old man what his plans are for the future, and he says, 'I don't know,' or, 'Right now I am in charge of peeling onions down at Billy-Bob's

Burgers and Biscuits, and that seems to be going good for me; next week I'm getting promoted to French fries,' RUN! RUN as fast as you can!" I am not saying there is anything wrong with working in fast food. My brother has managed fast-food restaurants for thirty years and has made a good, honest living with a good income. I am saying a young man should have some goals and plans for his future. He should have some ideas about how he is going to provide for a wife and children, and whatever he chooses to do, he should do it to the best of his ability.

Is This Person a Good Steward?

Moreover it is required in stewards, that a man be found faithful. (1St Corinthians 4:2)

The word *"steward"* implies someone who manages, keeps, provides or oversees. Good stewardship over personal matters in life is an important characteristic of which all Christians should be mindful. In the Bible, God commends good stewardship and warns of the dangers of poor stewardship. In considering someone for courtship and marriage, it would be in your best interest to observe a person's stewardship principles and practices. How well does he handle his money? Is he thrifty, or does he spend money unwisely? Is he careful to pay his bills, or is he irresponsible? Does he try to put money back for a rainy day or a future purpose, or does he make purchases on impulse, giving no regard to future concerns? In financial matters, these questions would be important for a young lady to think about, because the husband is usually the primary money earner in the marriage. A man should consider how a young lady handles money and views financial matters, because if she is not careful with the household budget and misuses the income, it could mean disaster.

There are other areas of stewardship that should be considered, such as how well this person takes care of the things he has worked for or the things that have been entrusted to him, such as automobiles, clothing, responsibilities in his job. Is he a good worker? Does he take his employment seriously, giving it his best effort in doing the job assigned to him by his employer?

Is he a good student? Does he strive to take advantage of the educational opportunities offered to him? What about his time? How does he spend it? What about the talents with which God has blessed him— is he nurturing and developing them? Is he a good steward for his relationships with family and friends? Does he cherish and nurture his most important relationships? The one thing that will give an understanding to all other areas of stewardship has to do with his testimony! Is he a good steward for his personal testimony? Is he a good steward of himself?

As our scripture tells us, *"Moreover it is required in stewards, that a man be found faithful."* Is this person a faithful steward of the things for which he is responsible?

Will This Person Make Me Complete?

And the LORD God said, It is not good that the man should be alone; I will make him a help meet for him....And Adam said, This is now bone of my bones, and flesh of my flesh: she shall be called Woman, because she was taken out of Man. Therefore shall a man leave his father and his mother, and shall cleave unto his wife: and they shall be one flesh. (Genesis 2:18,23,24)

Adam had the fellowship of all the animals of creation, and yet he was not complete. So, God created a helpmeet for him, a woman, a companion, a friend.

This woman became part of him, and he became part of her. The two became one. When you marry, you are no longer on your own; you are no longer just one. You have someone else who becomes part of your life.

Everything you do affects your spouse, and everything he or she does affects you.

The person you choose to marry should make you complete and help you complete your spiritual goals, your life goals. Your spouse should complete you in that he or she is God's will for your life. The goals for life, dreams, ambitions and philosophies of your spouse should blend with yours!

Will I Complete This Person?

Submitting yourselves one to another in the fear of God. (Ephesians 5:21)

Will you add to your spouse's spiritual goals? Will you complete his or her life goals? It is not only a matter of whether or not this person is right for you, but whether or not you are right for this person. Anyone who does not complete his or her spouse may be a hindrance instead. It is probably more important that the woman complete the man than that the man complete the woman. I realize that we are living in the twenty-first century and that some folks may not agree with this concept; however, God's plan in Scripture has been that the woman was made for the man. God created Eve to complete Adam.

God created the woman for the man. I don't want anyone to think I am picking on the ladies, so I will share some things with the men from Scripture. We read in Ephesians 5:25–28: *Husbands, love your wives, even as Christ also loved the church, and gave himself for it; That he might sanctify and cleanse it with the washing of water by the word, That he might present it to himself a glorious church, not having spot, or wrinkle, or any such thing; but that it should be holy and without blemish. So ought men to love their wives as their own bodies. He that loveth his wife loveth himself.*

Based on this Scripture, I believe the man makes his wife complete by loving her, by caring for the needs that she has as a woman and by helping fulfill her spiritual goals, life goals and the things for which God has created her. Verse 31 goes on to say, *"For this cause shall a man leave his father and mother, and shall be joined unto his wife, and they two shall be one flesh."*

Now let us consider what the Scriptures say about the woman's relationship to the man. Ephesians 5:21–23 says, *Submitting yourselves one to another in the fear of God. Wives, submit yourselves unto your own husbands, as unto the Lord. For the husband is the head of the wife, even as Christ is the head of the church: and he is the saviour of the body.*

Here again we see an example of the woman being created for the man. The church was created or instituted for Christ. Also, a married couple is to submit themselves to one another. This is part of the two becoming one, but we see specifically that the woman is to submit to the husband. When we consider this Scripture in light of our subject, I encourage any young lady considering a young man for courtship and possible marriage to ask herself if she believes she will complete the young man. I encourage a young man to ask himself the same question concerning a young lady.

What Do I Share in
Common with This Person?

Two are better than one; because they have a good reward for their labour. For if they fall, the one will lift up his fellow: but woe to him that is alone when he falleth; for he hath not another to help him up. (Ecclesiastes 4:9-10)

A couple does not have to agree on everything, and it is certain that they will not. They will not share all of the same interests; this is due in part to the fact that men and women are different. There are some things men enjoy that do not interest most women. Likewise, there are some things women enjoy that do not interest most men.

You do not have to have everything in common, but it is wise to understand what you do and do not have in common. For example, you may have grown up in a Christian home, while the person you are courting may not have grown up in a Christian home but has come to Christ and is now a faithful believer. There may be differences in social and financial backgrounds. I am not saying that these things should keep you apart or that they should keep you from courting someone to whom you feel led by God. I am saying that you need to understand the differences you may have because of these things.

It may be wise not to focus on what you do not have in common but what you do have in common. Interests in hobbies and recreation have their place of importance, but someone's spiritual beliefs and foundations, life goals, philosophy of family and child rearing are the most important things. I have always believed that God is more interested in your future than He is in your past.

The person in whom you have an interest may have a different past than you have, but if you can come to terms with that, if you have similar things in common now and if you have common goals for the future and common interests, you can build a lasting relationship.

You could develop an interest in the things you do not have in common. For example, a young lady may not have an interest in football, but the young man she is seeing enjoys attending and watching football games. A wise young lady will learn something about football and will develop an interest in it because it is important to her young man. On the other hand, a young lady may have an interest in flower gardens. This may not interest a young man, but the wise young man will learn about gardening and will develop an interest because the one he is fond of is interested in flower gardens.

Look at the things you have in common and consider their importance.

Can I Live for This Person?

"Intreat me not to leave thee, or to return from following after thee: for whither thou goest, I will go; and where thou lodgest, I will lodge; thy people shall be my people, and thy God my God." (Ruth 1:16)

I'm reminded of an illustration I heard a well-known evangelist's wife share. As I recall, she said, "When my husband and I were first married, we attended a family reunion on my father's side. While several of us were sitting outside enjoying the weather and talking among ourselves, my husband asked if I would get him a glass of iced tea. I got up from my seat, told him that I would go into the house to get it, and that I would be right back. A cousin who was visiting with us got up and followed me inside. When we got to the kitchen, my cousin barked, 'Is that it?" Is that how you're treated? Your husband wants a glass of tea, and you jump up and get it for him like some kind of servant?'

Without hesitation, I responded calmly yet boldly, 'I live to please my husband!'" What this precious evangelist's wife was saying to her cousin: "I live for my husband, and he lives for me. I treat him like a king, and he treats me like a queen."

Understand that when you marry, you no longer live for yourself—you live for your spouse. A man no longer works to provide for himself; in marriage he works to provide for his wife. A woman no longer lives for her own pleasure; in marriage she lives to please her husband. The two become one!

Will This Person Live for Me?

So ought men to love their wives as their own bodies. He that loveth his wife loveth himself. For no man ever yet hated his own flesh; but nourisheth and cherisheth it, even as the Lord the church. (Ephesians 5:28-29)

Probably the best way to analyze this question is to observe how the person you are courting treats others. Does he or she consider the needs of his or her parents or of others? Is the person selfish, thinking only of personal interests, or does he or she seek to meet the needs of others?

Is the one you are interested in considerate of your feelings, your physical and emotional well-being? Does he or she show an interest in your needs and try to share an interest in the things that concern you and interest you? Is this person sincere in conversations with you and with others? Does he or she express a genuine humility and a genuine consideration for the thoughts and interests of others? These are important things for you to consider, observe and ask yourself.

If you marry a person who lives only for himself or herself, you will have a lonely life; and if, when you marry, you do not live for your spouse, he or she will have a lonely life.

Would This Person Make a Good Parent?

Lo, children are an heritage of the LORD: and the fruit of the womb is his reward. As arrows are in the hand of a mighty man; so are children of the youth. Happy is the man that hath his quiver full of them: they shall not be ashamed, but they shall speak with the enemies in the gate. (Psalm 127:3–5)

One of the most important decisions a married couple will make is the way in which they will rear their children. One of the reasons it is such an important question is that disagreement about childrearing is one of the four major causes of marital problems. As a courtship becomes more serious and an engagement (betrothal) is considered, one of the things that should be discussed is children. The planning for children, the number of children, and parenting principles are all things that should be considered by couples contemplating marriage!

Observe how the person you are courting acts around children. Look for things like patience with them, enjoyment of their company, or negative remarks about children in general. Of course, everyone looks at other people's children differently than they do their own.

You may want to consider the kind of childhood the person you are courting had. If it was a bad childhood, does the person desire to provide a better childhood for his or her own children, or is baggage being carried that may influence his or her own parenting behaviors and skills?

You should both agree that you will rear your children according to the principles in the Word of God, bringing up your children "in the nurture and admonition of the Lord" (Ephesians 6:4).

I encourage any married couple who is considering having a child or is expecting a child to study what the Bible says about rearing children. They may want to purchase some good books on childrearing written by Bible-believing, experienced parents and read those books together.

One other piece of advice I give to a couple preparing for marriage is that they not have children right away. It is best first to get to know each other in the marriage relationship. If the two people are not well acquainted with each other and comfortable in their marriage, even a baby can be incorrectly looked upon as a burden instead of a blessing. God intended for children to be blessings!

Do I Know This Person Well Enough to Marry Him/Her?

Finally, be ye all of one mind, having compassion one of another, love as brethren, be pitiful, be courteous. (1St Peter 3:8)

Is there such a thing as "love at first sight"? Let me answer that question carefully. As teenagers, my wife and I met on two different occasions, to the best of our recollection. However, we did not realize we had met as teenagers until we had been courting for a while. As young adults, we met again when we were officially introduced to each other in the home of some mutual friends. That evening, we began to converse, and I soon believed in my heart that she was the one for whom I had been waiting. We soon began our courtship, which later led to our engagement and then to our marriage.

The way our society has denigrated courtship and marriage is grievous. Many couples today follow the philosophy of the Hollywood subculture. We hear today of couples meeting and then getting married within twenty-four to forty-eight hours. Of course, these marriages usually only last about forty-eight hours, which proves that you will only get out of a relationship what you invest in it.

It is wise to have a long courtship and a short engagement. The purpose of the courtship is so that a couple can get to know each other and so they can prepare for their marriage and their future together.

The purpose of the engagement is to begin preparing for the wedding. We need to grasp the idea that planning for the marriage is far more important than planning for the wedding.

The wedding will only last about an hour; the marriage is supposed to last a lifetime. You would not take a boat on a long voyage in the ocean without knowing something about the boat. You would want to know the reputation of its builder, the materials with which it was constructed, how the boat had been serviced, how it had been treated and cared for, as well as how it would hold up in a storm or dangerous turbulence. You would want to know as much as you could about the boat, its captain and its crew. Getting married is a long voyage, and in some ways it is unfamiliar territory. At times there are storms and turbulence. Marriage is far more important than an ocean voyage, and one should know all he can about the person with whom he is considering taking the lifetime voyage.

Many of the questions suggested in this book will help you get to know the person you are courting or considering but allow me to give you a few reminders.

Know as much as you can about his or her spiritual condition, history, family, testimony, interests, future plans, strengths and weaknesses. The time of courtship should be used to get to know each other, to become friends and to learn what you have in common with each other. The more careful you are in getting to know each other before you launch into marriage, the more you will enjoy the voyage together.

Am I in Love with This Person?

"The watchmen that go about the city found me: to whom I said, Saw ye him whom my soul loveth? It was but a little that I passed from them, but I found him whom my soul loveth: I held him, and would not let him go, until I had brought him into my mother's house, and into the chamber of her that conceived me." (Song of Solomon 3:3-4)

"Charity [love] suffereth long, and is kind; charity envieth not; charity vaunteth [boasts] not itself, is not puffed up, Doth not behave itself unseemly [shamefully], seeketh not her own, is not easily provoked, thinketh no evil; Rejoiceth not in iniquity, but rejoiceth in the truth; Beareth all things, believeth all things, hopeth all things, endureth all

things. Charity never faileth: but whether there be prophecies, they shall fail; whether there be tongues, they shall cease; whether there be knowledge, it shall vanish away.... And now abideth faith, hope, charity, these three; but the greatest of these is charity [love]." (1St Corinthians 13:4–8,13)

This topic brings to mind one of the reasons I believe it is unwise for young teenagers to get emotionally involved with someone of the opposite sex in a boyfriend/girlfriend relationship. To begin with, they are too young to prepare for marriage. Second, their intentions in having a "relationship" are not right.

Third, in most cases they do not have the emotional maturity to be in love. Please understand that I am not saying they do not have feelings, that they do not have sincerity and that they do not have love to give. I am saying that the emotional maturity level of a thirteen-year-old is not ready for a committed emotional relationship.

The stage of life at thirteen through eighteen is not a reasonable time to be seriously seeking a spouse.

So, what is it to be in love? The woman in our text asks the question, *"Saw ye him whom my soul loveth?"* She did not ask, "Have you seen him who is handsome?" or "Have you seen him who is the captain of the football team?" There is nothing wrong with being handsome or having athletic ability; the point is that this lady was looking for the man whom her soul loved. True love that comes from the soul goes beyond physical attraction.

The soul is that part of you which enables you to communicate. Soul love is when you love someone for what he is as a person; you love his gentleness, personality and outlook on life. I repeat, soul love is not physical attraction; it goes beyond that. It loves the person within. Love is not an infatuation. It is not dirty or selfish. Love does not take from purity; love rejoices in purity. Love does not seek for itself; love seeks after another! Love does not take; love gives!

In any relationship, but especially in the marriage relationship, love is the thing that will keep you going when all else fails.

When health is gone, love will suffer long; when mistakes are made, love will be kind. Love will not complain and grumble but will seek to help another rise to higher and better things. When financial hardships come, love will hope and endure; and when good things come— blessings of health, finances and strength—love will remain the greatest possession. When the twilight years come upon us, and when all the physical and material things seem to fade away, love will bear us up. Love will believe, love will hope, and love will endure.

How do we know when we are in love—soul love? Here are some basic characteristics of a relationship when soul love is present:

- When we are friends, but more than friends

- When we are like brother and sister, but more than brother and sister

- When we know someone's weaknesses and look beyond them

- When we know someone's faults and look past them

- When our attraction goes beyond what the eye can see to what the soul desires

- When we know someone's shortcomings and desire to make him or her whole

- When we are apart, our souls long to be together

- When we find that we can be content in the presence of the one whom the soul loves

- When it becomes obvious to others that our heart is fixed on someone whom we believe God has sent into our lives

- When we feel in our soul that there is no longer a need to search for another

• When we see that person as the one God has sent to make us complete and we believe that we will complete that person Then it is very possible that we may be in love!

Am I Ready to Make a Lifelong Commitment to This Person?

"Therefore shall a man leave his father and his mother, and shall cleave unto his wife: and they shall be one flesh." (Genesis 2:24)

When you enter into the bonds of marriage, you are no longer your own. You become one with another. As the text states, you leave your parents and cleave to your spouse; you become one flesh! Marriage is a commitment, one that God intended to last for the rest of your lives. Marriage is giving yourself daily to your spouse for the rest of your life. When you are courting, at the end of the day you return to your own place of residence, with your own personal material items. In marriage you share things in common with someone else.

You adjust to the likes and dislikes of your spouse. In marriage you will find some habits that your spouse has that you may not have known about before marriage and some of these habits may irritate you. But when these habits come to mind, you must remember that you are committed.

I have heard people receive counseling for marriage problems that suggested the person "be committed to the marriage" or "remain committed to the marriage, because you can work it out." Well, I agree marriage problems can generally be worked out if both parties are willing; however, I believe the best advice is to be committed to your spouse, the person to whom you are married. The wedding vows are not a commitment to a marriage but a commitment to the person whom you marry. So, as you contemplate marrying, carefully consider and ponder this very important thought: You are making a commitment to a person, a person you believe God has sent to you! This is a person about whom you believe the following: you share things in common, he or she will make you complete, you are in love with each other; you want to spend the rest of your life together; you want to grow old together. MARRIAGE IS ABOUT MAKING A COMMITMENT TO A PERSON FOR THE REST OF YOUR LIFE!

Am I Ready for the Responsibilities of Marriage?

For which of you, intending to build a tower, sitteth not down first, and counteth the cost, whether he have sufficient to finish it? Lest haply, after he hath laid the foundation, and is not able to finish it, all that behold it begin to mock him, Saying, This man began to build, and was not able to finish. (Luke 14:28–30)

She considereth a field, and buyeth it: with the fruit of her hands she planteth a vineyard.
(Proverbs 31:16)

As we have already discussed, marriage is the second most important decision you will ever make. It is secondary only to receiving the Lord Jesus Christ as your Saviour.

It seems that today many young couples spend months planning their wedding but no time at all to plan their marriage. They do not consider the tremendous responsibility that comes with marriage. Now don't get me wrong. There are tremendous blessings that come with marriage, but with blessings there are also responsibilities. Pastors, parents and others involved in the lives of those planning a wedding share in the task of helping young couples consider and understand the responsibilities that come with marriage. They must also help them see that more emphasis should be placed on the planning of the marriage than on the planning of the wedding!

Sir Winston Churchill said, "The price of greatness is responsibility." To paraphrase Mr. Churchill's statement, marriage is great, but it comes with responsibilities!

In Luke, chapter 14, the Saviour gives the parable of a man who began to build a tower without considering the cost of the materials necessary to finish it. It is my desire that you find the person God has for you to marry, that you plan your wedding well, and that you plan your marriage even better so you can finish it.

Many marriages end in failure today for the simple reason that the couples planned a wonderful, beautiful and often elaborately expensive wedding, but they did not count the cost of the marriage. They did not take into consideration the responsibilities that come with the marriage.

For the husband, there will be the primary financial responsibilities. So, the man should be secure in his career plans. He should realize that after marriage a child could soon become part of the family, and he should be prepared to accept that responsibility.

I realize that today many marriages have both the husband and wife in the work force, and I understand that.

However, I have always believed it is best if the wife is able to stay home when children enter the family so that she can care for them. This is part of the responsibilities of marriage, and the topics of both spouses working and child rearing should be prayerfully discussed as young couples are planning their marriage.

A man must also understand upon entering the marriage that his wife will take priority over his old friends in the "old gang". She will want him to be home with her and not out at the bowling alley or at the park playing ball all the time. She will desire his company. She will desire and need his attention.

Ephesians 5:25,26 says, *Husbands, love your wives, even as Christ also loved the church, and gave himself for it; That he might sanctify and cleanse it with the washing of water by the word.*

A wife wants her husband to give himself in conversation with her. She wants her husband to give himself in helping with the responsibilities of maintaining the home and the relationship. In my years of marriage counseling, I have found that one of the biggest criticisms women have of their husbands is that they do not communicate; that is, they do not give themselves to their wives in conversation.

The husband will also need to understand that his wife will expect him to provide for her, to give her financial security, to manage the income and the budget of the marriage, to be responsible with the finances.

Consider the example of Isaac. When Isaac took Rebekah to be his wife, he provided a home for her.

Genesis 24:67 tells us, *And Isaac brought her into his mother Sarah's tent, and took Rebekah, and she became his wife; and he loved her: and Isaac was comforted after his mother's death.* It is interesting to note that Isaac provided a home for Rebekah. He married her, he loved her, and he was comforted. Isaac provided Rebekah's need for financial security; he also provided Rebekah's emotional security in that he loved her.

Through Isaac's providing of Rebekah's needs, she was able to provide his need to be comforted.

The point is that if the man will strive to take care of his wife's needs in marriage, it will be natural for the woman to take care of her husband's needs. It has been my experience in years of counseling married couples that when the wife does not feel her husband is performing his responsibilities in the marriage, i.e., providing financially and emotionally for his wife, then the wife will feel insecure and unloved.

I encourage any young couple preparing for marriage to learn how to make a budget and manage their finances. I also encourage young men preparing for marriage to have a savings account with at least three to six months of income in the bank. This will be very reassuring to a young woman that her man is responsible and will provide security for her.

The husband should realize that God intended him to be the spiritual leader in the home. He should lead in family devotions and be faithful to church and to the Bible. In his prayer life, he must seek the Lord's direction in his marriage and family.

The wife needs to understand that her first responsibility is to her husband. In Genesis 3:16, God told Eve, *"Thy desire shall be to thy husband, and he shall rule over thee."* The thought I want to get across is that the wife's desires should be to and for her husband. He will have physical needs, and he will want those needs fulfilled by his wife. In the man's mind, the wife's most important responsibility in the marriage is to fulfill his physical needs.

A young woman soon to be married should not be shy about asking questions of a godly woman or her pastor's wife as she begins premarital counseling. Titus 2:3–5 tells us, *"The aged women likewise, that they be in behaviour as becometh holiness, not false accusers, not given to much wine, teachers of good things; That they may teach the young women to be sober, to love their husbands, to love their children, To be discreet, chaste, keepers*

*at home, good, obedient to their own husbands,
that the word of God be not blasphemed."*

It is very wise for a young woman to seek the counsel of a godly married woman before approaching the marriage altar.

A young woman preparing for marriage should understand that her future husband will want her attention and will desire her encouragement. She has great power with him just in the words she speaks to him.

She even will have the power to make him a better man with her words of encouragement. Proverbs 31:26 says, *She openeth her mouth with wisdom; and in her tongue is the law of kindness."* I cannot stress enough to a young woman how important her words are. It has been said that behind every great man stands a great woman. I believe that statement, but to paraphrase it, behind every happy contented man stands a woman cheering him on with words of encouragement and affection!

The married life can be a wonderful and fulfilling one, but there are many responsibilities that come with marriage. In this book, I have attempted to point out some of those responsibilities. I encourage the young person considering marriage to discuss carefully and contemplate the responsibilities of marriage and to seek counsel together with his or her future spouse in planning their marriage even more fervently than they do their wedding.

Holy and Beautiful
Intimate Life in Marriage

Let the husband render unto the wife due benevolence: and likewise also the wife unto the husband. 4) The wife hath not power of her own body, but the husband: and likewise also the husband hath not power of his own body, but the wife." (1 Corinthians 7:3-4) The Sacred Scriptures teach that the sexual union between a husband and wife is Holy and Beautiful.

Christians need to unlearn some false teachings about the sexual union of marriage. The idea that physical intimacy in marriage is dirty and is only about the man's animal passions is not what the Bible teaches.

The sexual union in marriage is Holy in that it was and is ordained of God; it is Holy in that it is set apart for the marriage bond only. It is Holy in that it's God's design for replenishing the earth, giving God more people to love.

In creation, the only thing that God said was *"not good"* was for man to be alone. In his book, [4]"The Ministry of Marriage" my friend Dr. Jim Binney

---

[4] The Ministry of Marriage, Dr. Jim Binney Faithful Life Publishers; Illustrated edition (November 28, 2014)

writes, "The first mention of a truth in Bible interpretation is of great significance in determining the importance of that doctrine. Notably, the first and second mentions of marriage refer to physical union. *"...Be fruitful, and multiply, and replenish the earth, and subdue it: and have dominion over the fish of the sea, and over the fowl of the air, and over every living thing that moveth upon the earth."* (Genesis 1:28) *24) Therefore shall a man leave his father and his mother, and shall cleave unto his wife: and they shall be one flesh. 25) And they were both naked, the man and his wife, and were not ashamed.* (Genesis 2:24-25) The emphasis is fruitfulness, oneness of flesh, and disallowance of shame. Interesting choice of words, don't you think, *"and were not ashamed."?* Apparently, God wants us to know that there is nothing shameful about the oneness of marriage. Indeed *"marriage is honourable in all"* (Hebrews 13:4)

Dr. Binney reminds us that the first thing God told a married couple to do was to *"...Be fruitful, and multiply, and replenish the earth, and subdue it..."* To be fruitful means, "prolific, bearing children". To multiply means to, "grow or increase in number." To replenish is "to stock with numbers or abundance." God created the sexual union between a husband and a wife as the means to accomplish this. This is the Holiness and Beauty of the sexual relationship between a husband and wife.

Dr. Binney writes, "During the sexual union, you become one with your spouse, literally becoming "one flesh" (Genesis 2:24). This union of two is more than that of two bodies; it is a cleaving, a knowing, a bonding of two personalities much like that of the inseparable union of the Godhead."

God intended the sexual relationship between a husband and wife to be physical, emotional, and spiritual. Let's begin with the spiritual beauty; a man and a woman come together in marriage as God designed in the beginning. Creating the woman for the man because *"...it is not good that the man should be alone."* (Genesis 2:18). The sexual relationship in the bond of marriage is spiritual in that God likens marriage to the New Testament Church; *Husbands, love your wives, even as Christ also loved the church, and gave himself for it;* (Ephesians 5:25) The sexual relationship in the bond of marriage is spiritual because when a husband and wife love the Lord Jesus Christ together and serve Him and live to bring their children up *"...in the nurture and admonition of the Lord"*; making their relationship more meaningful and their sexual relationship more meaningful.

The emotional beauty of the intimate relationship in marriage is that a man and woman have decided to love one another as husband and wife; they have made a commitment to one another and to God that they will be faithful and serve one another and become one in marriage spiritually, emotionally and physically.

The physical beauty is that they come together to please and enjoy one another in the physical marriage relationship as God designed it. This is Holy and Beautiful because God designed it to be between a husband and wife who have saved themselves for their spouse.

Toy or Treasure
A Message by Dr. Don Woodard
(Edited for Publication)
Delivered at Heritage Baptist Church
Crestline, Ohio–Pastor Rodney Noblit

Please find in your Bible the Book of Proverbs, chapter 31. We will begin our reading at verse 10 and read down through verse 28.

"Who can find a virtuous woman? for her price is far above rubies. The heart of her husband doth safely trust in her, so that he shall have no need of spoil. She will do him good and not evil all the days of her life. She seeketh wool, and flax, and worketh willingly with her hands. She is like the merchants' ships; she bringeth her food from afar. She riseth also while it is yet night, and giveth meat to her household, and a portion to her maidens. She considereth a field, and buyeth it: with the fruit of her hands she planteth a vineyard. She girdeth her loins with strength, and strengtheneth her arms. She perceiveth that her merchandise is good; her candle goeth not out by night. She layeth her hands to the spindle, and her hands hold the distaff. She stretcheth out her hand to the poor; yea, she

reacheth forth her hands to the needy. She is not afraid of the snow for her household: for all her household are clothed with scarlet. She maketh herself coverings of tapestry; her clothing is silk and purple. Her husband is known in the gates, when he sitteth among the elders of the land. She maketh fine linen, and selleth it; and delivereth girdles unto the merchant. Strength and honour are her clothing; and she shall rejoice in time to come. She openeth her mouth with wisdom; and in her tongue is the law of kindness. She looketh well to the ways of her household, and eateth not the bread of idleness. Her children arise up, and call her blessed; her husband also, and he praiseth her."

Please turn to Ephesians, chapter 5. We will read verses 25–29. *"Husbands, love your wives, even as Christ also loved the church, and gave himself for it; That he might sanctify and cleanse it with the washing of water by the word, That he might present it to himself a glorious church, not having spot, or wrinkle, or any such thing; but that it should be holy and without blemish. So ought men to love their wives as their own bodies. He that loveth his wife loveth himself. For no man ever yet hated his own flesh; but nourisheth and cherisheth it, even as the Lord the church."*

By way of introduction, I would like to share with you where I first got the thought upon which I want to speak. Recently I preached a revival meeting at the Central Baptist Church in Belmont, New Hampshire, where Doug Conley is the pastor. There is a wonderful couple in that church named Bill and Roberta Taylor. The Taylors have studied marriage for over fifty years. They have helped countless couples and young people in the area of courtship and marriage-related issues. They shared this thought with me, and I thought it was a wonderful concept.

I'm challenged by this topic. It is one of the topics I taught in our Mending Women's Hearts meetings recently in Roanoke. In my introduction, I shared with the ladies that it might be more beneficial to them if I taught it to men. After the session, several ladies expressed that they wished someone had told them these things when they were teenage girls. It was also expressed that these thoughts would be helpful to men.

I began to pray about how I could apply this topic in a way that would benefit everyone. Ladies, keep in mind that you are hearing a man's perspective. I want to speak to you on this thought—Toy or Treasure.

Men View Toys and Treasures Differently

Most men were taught as boys that a toy is something to play with. Many of them had a toy pickup truck when they were little. All little boys like to play with toy pickup trucks, and big boys like real pickup trucks.

Amen! Most boys believe that if you get bored with a particular toy, you just move on to a different one. After all there are plenty of toys to play with. If you break it, you just discard it. But before discarding a toy that is broken, often a boy believes he should completely destroy it. After all, it doesn't work anymore, if it does not satisfy me anymore, if it does not work as I want it to, it is no longer of any use to me, so its only purpose now is for the child to get some pleasure out of it by totally demolishing it.

Before completely destroying a toy that does not work, the average boy will try a few other things. If the toy does not work properly, he will try yelling at it! If that does not bring satisfaction, he tries yelling at it again. If that does not produce the desired result, he can try hitting it, and of course, if that does not work, he can try hitting it again! If that does not work, he will abandon that toy for another toy.

There is usually no loyalty to toys because they can be easily replaced. Another reason there is little loyalty, if any, between a boy and his toys is the perception that a new model or new kind of toy is always on the market. His toy truck will soon be outdated, and if you go to the toy store you will find that there are rows and rows of shelves with brand–new models of toy trucks—brand-new ones with new and better features than the one he has.

 Boys usually do not take the best care of their toys because their perception is that:

 • Toys are easy to come by—parents are always buying new ones.

 • Toys do not have feelings; after all, they are just toys, just mechanical objects.

 • Toys are made only for a boy's pleasure. If they cease to give pleasure, they are no longer necessary.

 • Toys are replaceable. The sad thing is that too often in our society, boys are taught that women are toys and not treasures.

Boys Are Taught Differently About Treasures

 My mother had what she called her "China Cabinet". It was not fancy, but she kept items in that cabinet that were valuable to her. She had some dinnerware that was more valuable than the normal dinnerware we used daily. She had some items in that cabinet that were "Pretty things". Items she valued, little gifts or items she had purchased because she admired them. Myself or my brother or sister were not permitted to touch the items in the "China Cabinet", they were mother's treasures.

Boys are usually taught that Mother's China is a treasure. They are told, "Don't touch it unless you have permission! If you do get permission to remove the China from the cabinet, do so very carefully." Most boys are told and believe, "The China is very valuable. It cost a lot of money! It is very fragile—It must be handled very carefully!"

Boys are always told, "Wash your hands. A boy should never touch the China with dirty hands!" In other words, "A boy should never touch the treasure with dirty hands!" Boys are sternly told, "CHINA CANNOT BE REPLACED! CHINA IS NOT A TOY!" To paraphrase, "THE TREASURE IS NOT A TOY!"

God Intended Women to Be Treasures, Not Toys! Scripture tells us that God created woman as a helpmeet for man. "Helpmeet" implies that she was to make man complete. A virtuous woman's price, her value, is far above rubies. Husbands are commanded to love and give honor to their wives.

Why Are Some Women Not Treated as Treasures?

It could be that men were not taught the difference between toys and treasures. Some men are not taught that there is a difference between playthings and fragile treasures.

Others, perhaps, had a bad example or no example at all to follow on how to treat a woman properly.

Eighteen million children in America do not have a father in their lives. Society portrays women as toys, not treasures. Pornography runs rampant; perversion and Hollywood movies have denigrated the sanctity of marriage.

Some women are not taught that they are supposed to be treated as a treasure. Incest and molestation are too common in our own nation and go unpunished.

A number of women do not believe that they are valuable and that they should be treated like treasures.

They were reared by men who spoke down to them, or who mistreated them by calling them names and by being vulgar toward them.

Often, women do not know how to present themselves as treasures. They do not know that it matters how they dress, how they walk and how they talk. They do not understand that most men view women as toys if the women see themselves as toys instead of treasures.

Some women will take negative attention over no attention at all. These women would rather be a toy than a nothing. They do not know that God intended them to be treasures, and they think that being mistreated is all there is for them.

Some Men Determine Whether a Woman Is a Toy or Treasure by How She Presents Herself

Many men will determine a woman's value by how she views herself, how she views her self-worth, her value as a person and as a companion! Often the way a woman dresses reveals to a man how she views herself. Treasures send a message by how they dress, and toys send the opposite message.

The average man interprets what a woman thinks about herself by her conversation. Most men view flirtatious women as toys. Men view women who use vulgar language as toys.

Ladies, some men interpret what you think about yourself by what you are willing to settle for.

How Can a Woman Detect When a Man Knows the Difference Between Toys and Treasures? How Can a Man Determine If He Knows the Difference?

First, does the man respect himself? The Bible tells us, *"So ought men to love their wives as their own bodies. He that loveth his wife loveth himself"* (Ephesians 5:28).

A man that does not take care of his own personal hygiene and is not willing to dress neatly does not respect himself. Generally, a man that does not respect himself will not respect others.

Second, how does he treat his mother? A man that does not show common courtesy and respect to his mother will not respect other women, and a man that mistreats his own mother will mistreat other women.

Third, does he keep his commitments? Does he keep his word? Does he do what he says he is going to do? If he does not keep his word in little things, he will not keep his word in the more important matters of life.

Ladies, what about the respect factor? Does he compliment your appearance without being vulgar? When he greets you, does he do so like he is taking China from a cabinet, or like he is taking a toy from a toy box?

Making Application

I begin with adult men! We have a great responsibility to teach young men by example the proper way to treat women. We must treat our wives like treasures!

We must be pure in our relationships with them! We need to determine in our hearts that we are going to treat our wives right—like treasures, not toys! We must also determine to guard our thoughts toward women.

Young men, you can start by treating your mother like she is a treasure. Understand that no young lady is your personal property. Learn that girls are not toys and that God intended for you to treat them like treasures—to treat them with respect and honor. Until you are married, that Christian girl is God's property, not yours. God created you to treat her like a treasure, not a toy. Young men need to stay pure and keep their intentions pure!

Ladies, God intended for you to be treasures. Present yourself as a treasure! Make yourself valuable to your husband. Believe in your heart that no matter what your past has been, God created you to be treated like a treasure.

Present yourself that way and strive to be a treasure to your own husband.

Young ladies, God intended for you also to be treasures.

Be careful with your heart. Don't give your heart too soon, and don't give it to just anyone, and by all means don't give it to everyone. Present yourself as a treasure! You make a statement by how you dress and by how you walk and talk.

If you want a young man someday to treat you like you are a treasure, like you have great value, as a young woman to be cherished and adored, then be a treasure and not a toy.

Purpose in your heart to keep your purity! Determine that on your wedding day, you will present yourself, before God, pure to your groom. You are a treasure!

The Wedding Vows

"Submitting yourselves one to another in the fear of God."—Ephesians 5:21.

The wedding vows are very precious, and as we discussed earlier, they consist of a commitment two people make to each other. These vows should not be taken lightly, and the pastor should carefully discuss their importance in premarital counseling.

The following are sample wedding vows. As you read through them, consider their importance, and consider also the commitment that is made when they are spoken on your wedding day.

Vows

If you, [groom's name], and you, [bride's name], have freely and deliberately chosen each other as partners for life, would you please join right hands.

[Groom's name], will you have this woman to be your wedded wife? Will you love her, honor and keep her in sickness and in health, in poverty and in wealth, and, forsaking all others, keep thee only unto her so long as you both shall live? Do you promise? [Groom's response "I do."]

[Bride's name], will you have this man to be your wedded husband? Will you love him, honor and keep him in sickness and in health, in poverty and in wealth, and, forsaking all others, keep thee only unto him so long as you both shall live? Do you promise? [Bride's response "I do."]

[Groom's name], would you repeat after me the following words, please?

I, [groom's name], take thee, [bride's name], to be my wedded wife, to have and to hold from this day forward, for better, for worse, for richer, for poorer, in sickness and in health, to love and to cherish, 'til death do us part.

[Bride's name], would you repeat after me the following words, please?

I, [bride's name], take thee, [groom's name], to be my wedded husband, to have and to hold from this day forward, for better, for worse, for richer, for poorer, in sickness and in health, to love, cherish and obey, 'til death do us part.

Exchange of Rings

With this ring I thee wed, pledging all my love to thee. [Repeated for each]

What God hath joined together, let not man put asunder.

Prayers, Dreams and Time

(For my daughters: April, Amber and Jennifer
For my nieces: Patsy and Lauren)

Will I be your hero, little girl of mine?
I hold you in my arms today,
With visions of what may be,
With prayers, dreams and time.

Am I your knight in shining armor?
Your doll baby's arm I have mended.
And carefully laid her in the crib,
Having placed a kiss upon her brow.

Am I still your hero?
Now a two-wheeler you can ride.
You are still my little girl of prayers, dreams and time.

Am I still your hero?
Other friends you have met.
I did not know the age of ten could come so quickly, Little girl of mine, with prayers, dreams and time.

Am I still your hero, now that you're a teen?
Baby doll lies quiet and still in her little crib,
Uncared for, it seems. You remain my little girl.
Of prayers, dreams and time.

Am I still your hero? High school days are here. You have dreams and fears which I too long to share. You are still my little girl.
Of prayers, dreams and time.

Am I still your hero as you graduate from school?
I once had visions of all you are today,
Bright, beautiful and full of life
With prayers, dreams and time.

Am I still your hero, as off to college you have gone?
Books, a boy and studies too; your life is so busy,
All grown up it seems. But you are still my little girl of prayers, dreams and time.

Am I still your hero?
The wedding march I hear them play.
I will walk you down the aisle soon; your hand in his I'll place.
I once had visions of all you are today,
Through prayers, dreams and time.

Am I still your hero?
Your heart you now give to him.
And I confess my heart does ache; Yet I remember when I held you in my arms, Little girl of mine.
In my heart, I had visions of all you are today.
Yet you will always be My little girl,
Through prayers, dreams and time.
—Dr. Don Woodard
May 25, 2001

The Best Relationship

Have you ever considered the importance of your relationships? And have you ever considered how our relationships affect our lives? Life is about relationships, most of your blessings in life are connected to a relationship and most of your challenges are connected to a relationship.

There is one relationship that excels above all other relationships and that is our relationship with God through His only begotten Son Jesus Christ. God created us for the purpose of a relationship, and He created you personally for the purpose of a relationship with Him. In John 17:3 as Jesus prayed to God the Father, He stated his purpose in coming to earth ...that they might know thee the only true God, and Jesus Christ, whom thou hast sent.

God loves you!

John 3:16 tells us *For God so loved the world, that he gave his only begotten Son, that whosoever believeth in him should not perish, but have everlasting life.* This verse assures us of God's love for us!

1st John 4:10 says, *Herein is love, not that we loved God, but that he loved us, and sent his Son to be the propitiation for our sins.*
God expressed His love for you by sending Jesus Christ to be our sin sacrifice on the Cross.

The first humans, Adam and Eve disobeyed God and sinned against Him, bringing the curse of sin upon the entire human race. God still loves us, and He desires a relationship with us even though we fail Him, and we sin.

God Loves You Unconditionally

Romans 5:8 says, *But God commendeth (committed) his love toward us, in that, while we were yet sinners, Christ died for us.*
God proved His unconditional love to you with the death of His Son Jesus Christ on the Cross. While suffering on the Cross Jesus Christ shed His blood and gave His life so that every sin you and I have ever committed or will ever commit could be forgiven and so you could have a personal relationship with Him.

Jesus Christ invites you to come to Him

Mathew 11:28-30 says, *Come unto me, all ye that labour and are heavy laden, and I will give you rest. Take my yoke upon you, and learn of me; for I am meek and lowly in heart: and ye shall find rest unto your souls. For my yoke is easy, and my burden is light.*

What a wonderful invitation from Jesus! He invites you to enter into a relationship with Him wherein He will give you rest from the challenges of life, share your burdens, encourage your heart and give rest to your soul. It is a peaceful and wonderful thing to know that God has forgiven us of our sins and that we are going to Heaven at the end of our lives here on earth. But our relationship with God also includes the present. In your relationship with God, you have Someone you can go to with life decisions, someone who loves you unconditionally who wants to share your burdens. In Jesus Christ you have a True Friend that will never leave you or forsake you. In Him you have a friend you can converse with daily, and yet He is not just anyone; He is the creator of the universe, He is the one who created you for the very purpose of having a relationship, the best relationship you could ever have.

Jesus Christ initiated the Relationship

Jesus took on the form of humanity; He came to earth and lived a life of service and sin-less-ness. Through His miracles He proved that He is the Son of God and the most important miracle of all was when He willingly went to the Cross to shed His blood and die for our sin. After his death He was buried and three days later He was resurrected from the dead and became very much alive. He did all of this to demonstrate to you that God desires a relationship with you. God reached out His hand through His Son Jesus, to invite you to enter into a personal relationship with Him. Will you respond to God's invitation to have a relationship with Him?

Here is How You Can Respond to This Invitation:

Believe

In John 5:24 Jesus said, *"Verily, verily, I say unto you, He that heareth my word, and believeth on him that sent me, hath everlasting life, and shall not come into condemnation; but is passed from death unto life."*

Romans 10:9-10 says, *That if thou shalt confess with thy mouth the Lord Jesus, and shalt believe in thine heart that God hath raised him from the dead, thou shalt be saved. For with the heart man believeth unto righteousness; and with the mouth confession is made unto salvation.*

Like other relationships our relationship with God begins with us trusting Him, by believing that Jesus Christ is the Son of God, believe that He loves you, that He shed His blood on the Cross and died for your sins and rose again three days later.

God does not expect us to understand all of this, but He does ask us to trust Him, to believe in Him and His Son Jesus Christ.

Turn to God

The Bible word is "repent" which means that we realize we have trespassed against God with our sin and that we are sorry for our trespasses. It also means that we now want to turn from our sin and ourselves and turn to God. To repent is to change our mind and direction from ourselves to a relationship with God through Jesus Christ.

I offer this example: When I met my wife Debbie, I had an interest in two other young ladies I was keeping company with. However, I did not see a future with either one of them even though they were nice girls. When I met Debbie, everything changed, I had a serious interest in her, so I turned from the other two and turned my heart and thoughts to Debbie completely, and we eventually married.

Repentance is turning from ourselves and our sin and turning to God for a relationship that is like no other relationship.

Confess

To confess means to acknowledge you have done something wrong.

Romans 10:9 says, *that if thou shalt confess with thy mouth the Lord Jesus, and shalt believe in thine heart that God hath raised him from the dead, thou shalt be saved.*

We enter into a relationship with God by acknowledging that we have trespassed against

Him and that we need His forgiveness, His salvation and Him.

<u>Believe with the sincerity of your heart!</u>

In Matthew 22:37 Jesus said, *"...thou shalt love the Lord thy God with all thy heart."* Romans 9:9 says, *"...and shalt believe in thine heart."*
Romans 10:10 says, *"For with the heart man believeth unto righteousness."*

This is an important matter in all our close relationships, and it is especially important in our relationship with God. The heart is our most inner being, it is the center of who we truly are.

The things we sincerely believe in our heart are the things we live by, they are the things that guide our decisions, and they are the things we grow by. Entering into a relationship with God is something that must sincerely come from your heart. It is more than saying a prayer; it is more than making a change in your life. A heart relationship with God is a transformation of your life through believing on Jesus Christ as your personal Saviour!

God invites you to enter into a relationship with Him through faith and I encourage you to turn to Him now, confess your sin to Him and believe on Jesus Christ with your heart.

<u>A Sample prayer of Salvation</u>

Dear God, I confess that I have sinned and trespassed against you; I now turn from myself and my sin and turn to you with my heart. I believe that you love me, and that Jesus Christ is your only begotten Son; and that He shed His blood and died on the Cross for my sins. I further believe that He was resurrected on the third day. I place my faith in Jesus Christ's finished work on the Cross for my personal salvation and for a personal relationship with you. Amen!

This is a model prayer; the most important thing is that you be sincere and believe in your heart on Jesus Christ.

Once you have believed on Jesus as your Saviour, you have then entered into a personal relationship with Him, and He has a relationship with you! This is the best relationship you will ever have. God bless you!

My friend, if you just prayed that prayer sincerely from your heart, please write to me. I would like to send you some free material that will help you.

Your friend,

Don Woodard

Life Relationships
PO Box 490
Troutville, VA 24175

Dr. Don Woodard
Liferelationships.net
➤ Revival Meetings
➤ Relationship Revival Sundays
➤ One Heart Marriage Seminars
➤ LightKeeper Publications
540-354-8573 / dr.donwoodard@gmail.com

Candlestick Light to Haiti
➤ Orphanage
➤ Children's Ministries
➤ Christian Education
➤ Equipping National Pastors
➤ Scripture Distribution

160

Made in the USA
Columbia, SC
26 March 2025

55733668R00098